The End of Jev

The End of Jewish Modernity

Enzo Traverso

Translated by David Fernbach

First published in French as *La fin de la modernité juive: Histoire d'un conservateur* by Editions La Découverte

English translation first published 2016 by Pluto Press
345 Archway Road, London N6 5AA

www.plutobooks.com

Copyright © Editions La Découverte, Paris, France, 2013;
English translation © David Fernbach, 2016

The right of Enzo Traverso to be identified as the author of this work and David Fernbach to be identified as the translator has been asserted by them in accordance with the Copyright, Designs and Patents Act 1988.

British Library Cataloguing in Publication Data
A catalogue record for this book is available from the British Library

ISBN 978 0 7453 3661 9   Hardback
ISBN 978 0 7453 3666 4   Paperback
ISBN 978 1 7837 1817 7   PDF eBook
ISBN 978 1 7837 1819 1   Kindle eBook
ISBN 978 1 7837 1818 4   EPUB eBook

This book is printed on paper suitable for recycling and made from fully managed and sustained forest sources. Logging, pulping and manufacturing processes are expected to conform to the environmental standards of the country of origin.

Typeset by Stanford DTP Services, Northampton, England

Simultaneously printed in the European Union and United States of America

Contents

Acknowledgements	vi
Introduction	1
1. What Was Jewish Modernity?	7
2. Cosmopolitanism, Mobility and Diaspora	20
3. Intellectuals Between Critique and Power	35
4. Between Two Epochs: Jewishness and Politics in Hannah Arendt	60
5. Metamorphoses: From Judeophobia to Islamophobia	82
6. Zionism: Return to the Ethnos	98
7. Memory: The Civil Religion of the Holocaust	113
Conclusion	128
Notes	133
Index	158

Acknowledgements

I've become aware in writing this book of my debt to many scholars, and would like to mention at least two of them here: Dan Diner, with whom every conversation is a source of enrichment and reflection, and Michael Löwy, who introduced and guided me through the study of Jewish history 30 years ago. He has become a friend and remains an indispensable interlocutor. I do not know how far either of them shares my hypotheses and interpretations, for which they of course bear no responsibility, but their help has been most valuable. The same holds also for Laurent Jeanpierre and Rémy Toulouse, who subjected my manuscript to a valuable critical reading. My thanks to you all.

Paris, Fall 2012

The English edition of this essay comes out three years after the original French. In the meanwhile, it has been translated into Italian and Spanish, and German and Turkish editions are forthcoming. As all scholars and public intellectuals know, an English translation is the necessary condition for reaching an international readership, and this is particularly true for a book devoted to Jewish history and culture in the twentieth century. Thus, I am very grateful to David Shulman for supporting this essay and allowing its release by Pluto Press, a publisher as scholarly rigorous as politically committed: a felicitous combination which I have always adopted as a model for myself. This English edition benefits greatly from the talents of David Fernbach, one the best translators working today, and I would like to thank him, too. In the countries where it already has been published, this book aroused controversies and criticism, was both enthusiastically received – including a prestigious award in Italy – and violently rejected. This is the destiny of all committed works, especially those that put into question commonplaces and contribute to destroying myths transformed into reasons of state. I hope this English edition will accomplish a similar role.

Ithaca, NY, February 2016.

Introduction

On 24 December 1917, Leon Trotsky, the newly appointed foreign minister of Soviet Russia, arrived at Brest-Litovsk for negotiations to be held with the Prussian empire in view of a separate peace. His delegation included a certain Karl Radek, Polish Jew and citizen of the Habsburg empire, wanted in Germany on account of his defeatist propaganda. As they got off the train, they began distributing leaflets to the enemy soldiers, calling for international revolution. The German diplomats observed them dumbfounded.[1] When they came to power, the Bolsheviks had made public the secret agreements between the tsarist regime and the Western powers; their aim was not to be accepted by international diplomacy but to denounce it. The state of mind of the German plenipotentiaries in the face of their Soviet counterparts is hard to comprehend today; we would have to imagine the arrival of an Al-Qaeda delegation at a G8 summit. Jews at this time were identified with Bolshevism, that is, a worldwide conspiracy against civilization. A bellicose conservative such as Winston Churchill saw them as 'enemies of the human race', representatives of an 'animal barbarism'. Civilization, he wrote, 'is being completely extinguished over gigantic areas, while the Bolsheviks hop and caper like troops of ferocious baboons amid the ruins of cities.' They destroyed everything in their path, 'like vampires sucking the blood of their victims'. Carried away by his eloquence, Churchill did not flinch from attributing Jewish traits to Lenin; this 'monster standing on a pyramid of skulls' was simply the leader of 'a vile group of cosmopolitan fanatics'.[2]

The wave of anti-Semitism triggered by the Russian Revolution did not stop short at Western diplomats. John Maynard Keynes, a member of the British delegation at the Versailles conference of 1919, described in striking terms the contempt that Lloyd George displayed towards Louis-Lucien Klotz, minister of finance in the Clemenceau government, who was particularly intransigent on the question of German reparations. Klotz, wrote Keynes, was 'a short, plump, heavy-moustached Jew, well groomed, well kept, but with an unsteady, roving eye'. In a fit of sudden and uncontrolled hatred, Lloyd George 'leant forward and with a gesture of his hands he indicated to everyone the image of a hideous Jew clutching a money-bag. His eyes flashed and the words came out with a contempt so violent that he seemed almost to be spitting at him. The anti-Semitism, not far below the surface in such an assemblage as that one, was up in the heart of everyone.' When the British prime minister called on his French opposite number to put an end to the obstructionist tactics of his finance minister, who, by his intransigence, risked playing the game of European Bolshevism alongside Lenin and Trotsky, 'All around the room you could see each one grinning and whispering to his neighbour "Klotzky".'[3]

Let us now jump forward half a century. On 27 January 1973, again in Paris, the representatives of the United States and the Democratic Republic of Vietnam signed a peace treaty at the end of another famous conference. The American plenipotentiary was Henry Kissinger, a German Jew who had emigrated in 1938, at the age of fifteen, to escape Nazi persecution. In this conference, however, the roles had changed. Kissinger did not represent revolution, but counter-revolution. It was he who, following his elevation to the State Department under President Nixon, had ordered the military escalation in Vietnam and Cambodia. Anti-war demonstrators across the world identified Kissinger with bombing and napalm. A few months after the Paris conference, Kissinger gave the green light to General Pinochet's putsch in Chile. The Nobel Peace laureate could boast of having organized several wars during his term at the State Department, some horrifically murderous, from Bangladesh to Vietnam, East Timor to the Middle East, as well as *coups d'état* from Chile to Argentina.[4] The hatred he aroused, deep as it was, had nothing in common with anti-Semitism, but rather with the rejection of what was now called imperialism.

Imperialism, indeed, was for Kissinger a kind of vocation. From the time of his studies at Harvard he identified with Metternich, the architect of restoration at the Vienna Congress of 1814, and above all with Bismarck, the builder of German unity, a statesman who saw international relations not in terms of abstract principles but rather of the balance of forces and *Realpolitik*. After the model of Bismarck, who had succeeded in 1871 in imposing Prussian hegemony in Europe by upsetting the balance of the concert of Europe, he saw himself as strategist of American hegemony in the world of the Cold War. Aware that power required self-restraint, Bismarck had been a 'white revolutionary', that is, a counter-revolutionary, capable of challenging the international order 'in conservative garb'.⁵ In the wake of Bismarck, Kissinger sought to be the embodiment of *Machtpolitik* in the second half of the twentieth century.

Trotsky and Kissinger: archetypes of the Jew as revolutionary and the Jew as imperialist. It is true that this opposition might need a certain qualification. On the one hand, a conservative Jewish diplomacy had already appeared in the nineteenth century, particularly in Great Britain and in France under the Third Republic, where the Alliance Israélite Universelle had a certain influence. On the other hand, there were still many Jewish revolutionaries in the 1960s and 1970s, particularly in France. The fact remains that Trotsky and Kissinger embody, beyond the chronological distance that divides them, two opposite paradigms of Jewishness. The first left its mark on the interwar years, the second on the years of the Cold War. This book sets out to study this change: its roots, its forms and its outcome.

Today, the axis of the Jewish world has shifted from Europe to the United States and Israel. Anti-Semitism no longer shapes national cultures, having given way to Islamophobia, the dominant form of racism in the early twenty-first century, as well as a new Judeophobia generated by the Israel-Palestine conflict. The memory of the Holocaust, transformed into a 'civil religion' of our liberal democracies, has made the former pariah people a protected minority, heir to a history providing a standard against which the democratic West measures its moral virtues. In parallel with this, the striking features of the Jewish diaspora – mobility, urbanity, textuality, extraterritoriality – have extended to the globalized world, normalizing the minority that formerly embodied them. It is Israel, on the other hand, that has reinvented the 'Jewish question' against the grain of Jewish history itself, in a statist and national form.

Jewish modernity, therefore, has reached the end of its road. After having been the main focus of critical thought in the Western world – in the era when Europe was its centre – Jews today find themselves, by a kind of paradoxical reversal, at the heart of the mechanisms of domination. Intellectuals are recalled to order. If the first half of the twentieth century was the age of Franz Kafka, Sigmund Freud, Walter Benjamin, Rosa Luxemburg and Leon Trotsky, the second half was rather that of Raymond Aron, Leo Strauss, Henry Kissinger and Ariel Sharon. It is possible, of course, to trace other trajectories, and mention in such varied fields the names of Claude Lévi-Strauss and Eric Hobsbawm, Emmanuel Levinas and Jacques Derrida, Noam Chomsky and Judith Butler, to show that critical thought does indeed remain a living Jewish tradition, with the capacity for renewal. But though this is undeniable (and reassuring), it is not enough to alter the general tendency. This metamorphosis did not take place without conflict and resistance, which continue today within a Jewish world that is in no way monolithic but remains very heterogeneous and complex. For example, many Jews still vote for the left, both in Europe and the United States, but this choice – often in the way of a tradition, an inherited culture – is no longer overdetermined by the particular position that they occupy in the social and political context. It is rather when they do not vote simply as American, French or Italian electors, but first of all as Jews, that their preference tends to go to political forces of the right. This is the conservative turn that the present book seeks to examine: its aim is neither to condemn nor to absolve, but to take account of an experience that is now at an end.

In many respects, this mutation of Jewish existence only follows a more general shift in the axis of the Western world. Why should Jews remain a focus of 'subversion' in a planet that has emerged from the Cold War, after the historical defeat of communism and the revolutions of the twentieth century? It is precisely by adapting to the chorus of the world that Jews have changed. They have become a mirror of general tendencies, whereas during the long wave of Jewish modernity they acted above all as a counter-tendency. Using a musical metaphor beloved of both Edward Said and Theodor W. Adorno, we could say that their voice, which used to be dissonant, is now in counterpoint. Today, it blends in with the harmony of the dominant discourse. The anomaly is over and exhausted, for better or worse.

Writing this book reawakened in me the memory of several inspiring individuals, now departed, whom I should like to remember here. Pierre Vidal-Naquet, who was a member of the jury for my thesis at the École des hautes études en sciences sociales (EHESS), in 1989, agreed to write a preface for this when it was published a year later. Soon after its acceptance, he presented me with the new edition of *L'affaire Audin*, his first book, thanks to which I discovered the commitment of Jews to the Algerian independence struggle.⁶ It was through Pierre's good offices that my book came to be read by the great Marxist Orientalist Maxime Rodinson (1915–2004), who wrote me a letter that was both critical and friendly. Soon after, I was contacted by some other remarkable people. First of all, Boris Frankel (1921–2006), to whom we owe the introduction of Freudo-Marxism into France, and who told me his colourful life story which is now the subject of a fine autobiography.⁷ A Jew from Danzig, he came to France as a refugee in 1939 and became a Trotskyist during the Second World War, in Switzerland where he had managed a further escape thanks to the complicit negligence of a French frontier guard. Expelled after the war, he remained stateless until the 1980s, when Mitterrand granted him French citizenship. In May 1968, General de Gaulle had tried to expel him to Germany, but his native country had no desire to welcome a stateless rebel and immediately returned him to France. He lived in great poverty, and devoted his leisure time entirely to exhibitions of painting. Germanophile in culture, like many émigré German Jews, he could not go without *Die Zeit* and the *Frankfurter Allgemeine Zeitung*. The affection with which he spoke to me of his exile friends, including Manès Sperber and Lucien Goldmann, helped me to understand Hannah Arendt's remarks on the human warmth of pariah Judaism. Finally, I heard from Jakob Moneta (1914–2012) in Frankfurt, whose very fine autobiography I was already familiar with.⁸ He had been victim of a pogrom in Galicia as a child, and came with his family to Germany as refugees, where he became a communist towards the end of the Weimar republic. After 1933 he moved to Palestine, but returned to settle in Cologne in 1948, critical of the foundation of the Israeli state: a remarkable choice at a time when Germany was still *terra non grata* for the World Jewish Congress. Attached to the German embassy in Paris in the 1950s, he used his diplomatic passport to take risks in supporting the Algerian Front de Libéracione Nationale (FLN). Moneta led me to discover another remarkable figure little known outside his own country: Sal Santen (1915–98). This Jew from Holland survived Auschwitz, where most members of his family were exterminated. In Amsterdam, where he lived as a journalist and writer, he was condemned in 1960 to two years in prison for his activities in support of the Algerian national movement. He had participated along with other anti-colonial activists in a network that concocted false papers, and in the establishment in Morocco of a small arms factory for the FLN. These men did not view themselves as 'victims', but as militants and committed intellectuals. I always had the impression that Jewishness for them was an *ethos*, an experience of the world, an existential commitment on the side of the oppressed. They defined themselves as internationalists, a word that for them had nothing abstract about it, but was how they had traversed their century of fire and blood. It is to their memory that I would like to dedicate the present book – a homage, I should add, that is more than just emotional; it also bears on a methodological choice. For various reasons, which relate to my education as much as my birth, my approach to Jewish history is strictly secular. I have passionately read Gershom Sholem and Yosef H. Yerusalmi, I admire their erudition and I have learned much from their works, with which it would be laughable to compare my own, but my view of history is significantly different from theirs, both in its motivations and its objective. I have never been interested in Jewish history as an object of study in itself. What is fascinating about it, to my mind, is the prism it offers for reading the history of the world. At the origin of my research, therefore, there is no quest of identity such as inspired Yerushalmi's vocation as a historian when he saw in the Boston Museum of Fine Arts Gauguin's painting entitled, *Where do we come from, where are we, where are we going?* In this sense, my book is simply another way of historicizing the twentieth century – an effort to which I have devoted other books as well – and beyond this, to question our own present.

I
What Was Jewish Modernity?

The concept of modernity has never enjoyed a clear and strict definition. Its meaning changes from one discipline to another, likewise its temporal divisions. It is more current in the field of literature and the arts than in that of historiography. Political modernity and aesthetic modernity are not simply different objects but also different epochs, even if there has always been some connection between the two. In this book, 'modernity' refers to a phase of Jewish history that is inextricably intertwined with history in general, and the history of Europe in particular. It includes various distinct dimensions – social, political, cultural – which, once again, have to be studied in their mutual relations. Historical periodizations, moreover, always arouse objections. In most cases they are approximate and unsatisfying. Periods are conceptual constructions, conventions, frames of reference rather than homogeneous temporal blocs. Epochs, like centuries, are mental spaces that never coincide with the divisions of the calendar. The same holds likewise for the boundaries of Jewish modernity. A posteriori, however, this appears in our historical consciousness as an epoch of extraordinary cultural richness with a well-defined and coherent profile, somewhat like Hellenism for Droysen, the Renaissance for Burckhardt or the Enlightenment for Cassirer.

According to the historian Dan Diner, Jewish modernity covers the two centuries from 1750 to 1950, from the beginnings of emancipation (the debate on the 'improvement' and 'regeneration' of the Jews) to the immediate aftermath of the genocide.[1] Prepared by the Enlightenment reformers, the decree voted by the French National Assembly in September 1791 set under way a process that, throughout the nineteenth century, transformed Jews everywhere in Europe into citizens – apart from in the tsarist empire, where this was delayed until the revolution of 1917. During the Second World War, the Holocaust violently broke what had seemed an irreversible tendency, then the birth of the state of Israel reconfigured the structure of Jewish modernity. This mutation was already prefigured at the start of the twentieth century, with the great transatlantic migration of Jews from central and eastern Europe; Nazism accentuated it, provoking the exile of German-speaking Jews (which some historians have interpreted as a gigantic cultural and scientific transfer from one side of the ocean to the other);[2] finally, after the war, the exodus of survivors from the extermination camps completed the turn. The axis of the Jewish world was shifted in this way – demographically, culturally and politically – from Europe to the United States and Israel. On the eve of the Second World War, almost ten million Jews had lived in Europe; by the mid 1990s less than two million remained.[3] After the war, Jewry practically ceased to exist in Poland, Ukraine, Lithuania, Germany and Austria, the countries that had been its main centres. On top of this, between 1948 and 1996 close to a million and a half Jews left Europe to settle in Israel,[4] which also received a massive influx (in equivalent proportions) of Jews from the Maghreb and the Near East, followed by Russian Jews. If the end of the Cold War did not mark a break comparable with that of the years 1945–50, it is because the decades that followed the fall of the Third Reich were those of the dissolution of the 'Jewish question' in Europe. The birth of Israel, on the other hand, generated a 'Palestinian question'. Europe became aware of the riches of a destroyed continent at the heart of its history and culture and sought to rescue this inheritance, but this rediscovery of its Jewish past inevitably crossed with the present of the Israeli-Palestinian conflict. Emancipation at one end, the Holocaust and the birth of Israel at the other, those are the historical boundaries that frame Jewish modernity. After having been its cradle, Europe became its tomb and its heir.

Emancipation led to an exit from the ghetto under a two-fold pressure: 'assimilation from without, collapse from within'.[5] It is true that Jews had played a far from negligible role since the Middle Ages, in culture as well as in the economy, being a major factor in the transmission of knowledge from philosophy to medicine. But emancipation secularized the Jewish world, breaking the walls that protected its particularism. By granting them the status of citizens, it forced Jews to rethink their relationship with the world around them.[6] The emancipatory laws, by carrying out the reforms projected by the Enlightenment in the late eighteenth century, put an end to a temporality of memory fixed by liturgy and plunged Jews into the new temporality of history, chronological and cumulative. Jewishness was steadily separated from Judaism, coming to be embodied in a new figure, that of the 'godless Jew' (*gottloser Jude*) or secular Jew, the definition of himself given by Freud.[7] Now emancipated, they became members of a political entity that transcended the borders of the religious community built around the synagogue; they ceased to be an *external* element, whether stigmatized or tolerated, persecuted or enjoying 'privileges' within society. Before this major turn they led a life apart, despite the generalized lack of political rights – their condition was certainly better than that of enserfed peasants. Accession to citizenship questioned the structure of their community life. From this turn on, the marginality of Jews was more a question of the attitude of the world around them than of their own desire to preserve a separate life. Modern anti-Semitism – the word appeared in Germany in the early 1880s – marked the secularization of the old religious prejudice and accompanied the whole trajectory of Jewish modernity as an insurmountable horizon, sometimes internalized, marking the limits to the dissolution of traditional Jewish communities. This is the source of the mixture of particularism and cosmopolitanism that characterizes Jewish modernity.[8]

During the 'long' nineteenth century, the Jews of western Europe became integrated into the national societies in which they lived, at the price of their collective and community rights (in Clermont-Tonnerre's famous formulations, the state must 'reject Jews as a nation' and 'grant everything to Jews as individuals').[9] This set under way a process of confessionalization, which relegated Jewishness to the private sphere, while the myth arose of Jews as a 'state within the state'.[10] They became 'Israélites' or 'of Mosaic faith' (*jüdischen Glaubens*). With its assimilation into national cultures, Jewishness metamorphosed into a kind of moral substratum, a 'spirit' that rabbis, scholars and notables celebrated as harmonizing with the various European nation-states, from the German Reich to the Habsburg empire, the French republic to the Italian monarchy. In eastern Europe, on the other hand, anti-Semitism posed an obstacle to emancipation. Here, the Jewish Enlightenment (*Haskalah*) appeared half a century later than in Berlin, Vienna or Paris, and took on a national form: secularization and modernization gave birth to a Jewish nation whose pillars were the Yiddish language and culture.[11] This was an extra-territorial community, as the historian Simon Doubnov has defined it, mingling with the people around it and sharing their own language (Russian or Polish), but with the addition of Yiddish, and certainly not sharing a national identity.[12] Tendentially, Jews remained a community apart, recognizable and distinct from others even if their life no longer (or not only) turned around religion.

The multinational empires of the nineteenth century – in which the *Ancien Régime* survived in modernizing societies[13] – formed propitious soil for the social and political integration of minorities. The specific features of the Jewish diaspora – textuality, urbanity, mobility, extraterritoriality – adapted better to these (despite tsarist anti-Semitism) than to nation-states.[14] The empires were far more heterogeneous than nation-states, in terms of ethnicity, culture, language and religion, and they tolerated (or even encouraged) the presence of diasporic minorities. Their dynastic legitimacy enabled them to perpetuate the principle of 'royal alliance': the submission of Jews to a protecting power that guaranteed freedom of trade and worship,[15] an old tradition that was only challenged by the advent of absolutism, followed by the nation-states of the nineteenth century. The nation, for its part, viewed every ethnic, linguistic or religious minority as an obstacle that it sought to overcome, by championing policies of assimilation or exclusion.[16] The retrospective and nostalgic idealization of the Habsburg empire that Stefan Zweig celebrates in *The World of Yesterday* (1942) is the best literary illustration of this love of European Jews for the liberal autocracies that came to an end with the First World War.

The urbanization of Europe gave rise to great metropolises in which Jews formed large minorities. The interstate networks they had established for more than a century had become one of the vectors of the continent's economic integration. Thanks to emancipatory laws, they experienced a marked rise, and the most powerful of their number were welcomed into the European elites. In France, a *haute bourgeoisie* business class existed already under the July monarchy and was consolidated under the Second Empire, when the Pereire brothers played a major role in the creation of a national railway network. In 1892, the 440 heads of financial establishments included close to 100 Jews.[17] In Germany, in 1910, the 600 richest taxpayers included 29 Jews. Jews were well established at the heart of the industrial, financial and commercial bourgeoisie. Similar tendencies were to be found at the same time in the Habsburg empire.[18] Their culture oriented to writing placed them at the centre of an emerging cultural industry, based around publishing and press. Journalism thus became a 'Jewish' profession, along with commerce and finance. But this was the Indian summer of the aristocracy in a dynastic Europe undermined by the rise of nationalisms, which revealed the fragility of emancipation. In fact, neither the historical experience of Jews nor their diasporic structure corresponded to the lexicon of political modernity, dominated by the triad of state, nation and sovereignty.[19] The concept of the 'Jewish people' defined a religious community and not an ethnic group, and when this people generated a national culture (of Yiddish language in central and eastern Europe), the latter presented a diasporic dimension that transcended state boundaries. This 'ambiguous semantics' inevitably came into conflict with the nation-states born from the treaty of Versailles in the wake of the collapse of the empires. In these states, Jews embodied modernity and polarized the rejection of conservative forces. In France, they became the target of legitimists and nationalists opposed to the Third Republic; in Italy, of Catholics horrified by the Piedmont monarchy that had led the peninsular's unification; in Germany, of conservatives who sought to preserve the Christian character of the Prussian monarchy. After 1918, Jews became a vulnerable minority that, deprived of the heterogeneous, multinational and multi-confessional space of the great empires, were perceived as a foreign body within the new states and exposed to the rise of nationalisms. They became the scapegoat of a European civil war that Nazi Germany brought to a paroxysmic expression.

In the wake of Hegel, for whom the absence of a state past characterized 'peoples without history', Ernest Renan termed the Jews a 'race' recognizable almost exclusively by 'negative features: no mythology, no epic, no science, no philosophy, no fiction, no visual artist, no civic life; in sum, lack of complexity and nuance, exclusive sentiments of unity'.[20] The final version of this thesis was that of the historian Arnold Toynbee who, in 1934, defined the Jews as a 'fossil' and 'petrified' diaspora, the survival of a bygone past.[21] We can understand the difficult task faced by scholars of the 'science of Jewry' (*Wissenschaft des Judentum*), from Nachman Krochmal, Leopold Zunz and Ludwig Geiger through to Heinrich Graetz, Moritz Güdemann and even Simon Dubnov, their Russian continuer, in demonstrating the existence of a Jewish history.[22] But their efforts came up against the incomprehension of national historiographies for which Jews were no more than an atavism in the modern world. The Jewish historiography of the nineteenth century abandoned the old theological viewpoint and replaced it with a new interpretation centred on a 'spirit of Judaism' that shaped a collective entity (Graetz's *Volksstamm*), whose accomplishments could be studied in economic, sociological and cultural terms. This collective entity, however, remained excluded from national status, which according to the Hegelian categories could only be granted by a state existence. Wavering between Fichte, Herder and Renan, Jewish nineteenth-century historiography could only conceive of the 'Jewish people' on a national model, by historicizing the biblical story.[23] This 'people' was conceived, in romantic terms, as a kind of innate entity, organic and timeless, whose history illustrated its fulfilment. Caught in the traps of emancipation, this historiography remained captive to its contradictions, despite its tremendous advances. Only Zionism managed to resolve it, by transforming the people of the Book into an ethno-cultural entity and its past into a national epic, through to its coronation as a state.[24]

Hannah Arendt, drawing on an intuition of Max Weber and Bernard Lazare, tackled the 'ambiguous semantics' of Jewish political history head-on in order to forge a new concept: pariah Judaism. Invisibility, exclusion from the public space and 'worldlessness' were for her its key features, despite the cultural richness it had demonstrated.[25] She set out on this basis to decipher totalitarianism by analysing its emergence as the product of the crisis of the system of nation-states. In a certain sense, Jewish modernity coincided with the trajectory of pariah Judaism. The obsession of Zionism, the child of nineteenth-century nationalisms, was to put an end to this 'ambiguous semantics', so that Jews would accede to a 'normal' existence: nation, state, sovereignty. Other thinkers, however, assumed this in order to shatter the political semantics of Western modernity itself, which for them was at bottom simply a system of domination. The characteristics indicated above (textuality, urbanity, mobility, extra-territoriality) formed the substratum of Jewish intellectual avant-garde. On the political level, they nourished the internationalism of Marx and Trotsky.

The Jewish anomaly thus lay at the heart of the tensions that marked the process of modernization in Europe throughout the nineteenth century, leading to its crisis between the two world wars. If Judeophobia has a millennial trajectory, anti-Semitism was born in the second half of the historical sequence noted above (1850–1950). During this period, the Jew embodied the abstraction of the modern world dominated by impersonal and anonymous forces. Mass society was perceived as a hostile realm shaped by big cities, the market, finance, the speed of communications and exchange, mechanical production, the press, cosmopolitanism, democratic egalitarianism, culture transformed into an industry by way of the press, photography and the cinema. Amid this upheaval, the Jew emerged as personification of a modernity in which everything was measurable, calculable and yet impossible to grasp, in which everything was removed from nature and annexed to the enigmas of an abstract and artificial rationality. As shown by a vast literature, from Georg Simmel to Moishe Postone, the Jew became a metaphor of the reified world, illustrating the fetishism of a social reality given over to monetary exchange and the phantasmagoria of the commodity.[26]

Anti-Semitism provided a way of rejecting this despised modernity despite a reconciliation with some of its aspects. Industry, trade and technology could be accepted and placed in the service of the concrete national community, rooted in a land, a culture and a tradition, after rejecting their abstract representation embodied by the Jew. Once the latter was eliminated, capital lost its parasitic character and became a productive force for the people. Anti-Semitism was thus one of the keys of a 'reactionary modernism' based on a synthesis of modern rationality and technology with the conservative values of the anti-Enlightenment.[27] In this perspective, the Holocaust was the most acute moment in a historical sequence marked by a discordance of timescales, by the violent confrontation between modernity and its rejection: the destruction of the Jews appeared as a liberatory fight against the group that embodied the abstraction of the modern world.[28] The transformation of Western societies in the latter part of the nineteenth century generated anti-Semitism. The subsequent European crisis exacerbated it, to the point of giving it an exterminatory dimension. The stabilization of the continent and the restoration of a new international equilibrium after 1945 finally began its decline.

One of the paradoxes of Jewish history – another source of its 'ambiguous' political semantics – lies in its relationship with the law. The latter, in the sense of the Mosaic law, was always the core of Jewish religion and culture, ensuring an internal cohesion that made up for the lack of political status. Emancipation granted rights to Jews as individuals, relegating the community to a purely religious existence deprived of any political prerogative. Under the tsarist empire, it was against the notion of a 'Jewish people' (which rather vaguely denoted the adherents of a religion across the world)[29] that the champions of cultural national autonomy such as Vladimir Medem demanded recognition of a Yiddish-speaking Jewish nation freed from its religious association.

A new paradox arose after the Second World War. On 9 September 1952, after three years of negotiations, the German Federal Republic, the state of Israel and the Conference on Jewish Material Claims Against Germany, represented by Nahum Goldmann, signed in Luxembourg the restitution (*Wiedergutmachung*) agreements which provided compensation for the victims of Nazi persecution, for Israel as the state that received the survivors of genocide, and for European Jewish communities who had suffered immense material losses (destruction of synagogues and religious objects, libraries, schools, retirement homes, etc.). They also concerned properties with no heirs, the goods of millions of exterminated Jews who could not claim any reparation. Often described as a symbolic act of recognition of 'German guilt' and of legitimation of the Federal Republic on the international stage (Adenauer's goal against a public opinion that still saw itself as a 'victim' of the war), these agreements marked a historic turning-point. The paradox lay in the fact that the two signature states, West Germany and Israel, did not yet have diplomatic relations, while the third signatory, the Claims Conference, was not a state at all. Born as an extension of *jus publicum europeum*, thus of the law of war, international law fixes the principle of reparations between states, not between states and individuals. The Luxembourg agreements thus constituted both an unprecedented event in legal history, being signed by a non-state institution (the Claims Conference was an offshoot of the World Jewish Congress), and an absolute first in Jewish history – recognizing that Jews (and not only citizens of Israel) belonged to a collective entity.[30] The 'Jewish people' suddenly acquired a legal and political dimension, and since these agreements also concerned goods without heirs, they erected this 'Jewish people' into a community of the absent. They could be symbolically interpreted as the start of a metamorphosis of Jews into a community of memory, united by the shadow of the Holocaust and no longer by the constraints of a law that had assured their continuity down the centuries. It was indeed as a collective entity that Jews had been persecuted by Nazism, no matter what their opinions, language and citizenship. The *Wiedergutmachung* agreements acknowledged this reality and materialized a 'Jewish people' that had ceased to exist; the nation that was in the process of formation in Israel saw itself precisely as a negation of the diaspora. Far from overcoming the ambiguities of Jewish political semantics, this posthumous recognition only shifted and renewed them.

A new cycle thus opened after the Second World War, in the wake of the Shoah and with the birth of the state of Israel. The extermination of the Jews, occurring as it did amid the violence of war, was not immediately perceived as a rupture of civilization, but the end of Nazism and its allies burst the abscess of anti-Semitism. Formerly a *nomos* of European nationalisms, and sometimes the cornerstone of the formation of national identity, as in Germany, anti-Semitism did not completely disappear; it was gradually transformed into *anomie*, in the Durkheimian sense, the result of a social breakdown that was regrettable but inevitable, and thus normal. In the same way as criminality, impossible to eradicate completely despite being punished by the law, anti-Semitism could be confined to 'tolerable' proportions.[31] Finally, it was the memory of the Holocaust, cultivated as a kind of civil religion of human rights, that resurrected a sense of community belonging among the Jews, by redrawing the profile of a minority that was no longer stigmatized. By undermining national sovereignties and making problematic the political categories inherited from the nineteenth century, globalization began to transform into a model of a diasporic minority whose existence had always been lived in urban centres, based on an international network and structured around exchange and communication (books, press, media). But globalization is only one side of the coin. The other is that of Israel, which has once again revealed the ambiguities of Jewish political semantics: the 'Jewish state' could only arise as a homogeneous nation-state by the exclusion of the Palestinians. To manufacture a new national entity, it had to root itself in a 'Jewish people' halfway between religious community and ethnos, at the moment when, in the Old World, national sovereignties were coming into crisis. In retrospect, this paradox seems highly symbolic. European construction began with the treaty of Paris in 1951, signed by West Germany, France, Italy and the Benelux countries, which established the European Coal and Steel Community. By their origins, their education and their culture, its architects saw frontiers as places of transition and encounter rather than separation. Chancellor Konrad Adenauer, the former mayor of Cologne persecuted by Hitler, embodied a Germany that was Rhenish, Catholic and Western, opposed to Prussian nationalism as well as Nazism. Robert Schuman, the French foreign minister, was born in Luxembourg and grew up in a Lorraine annexed by Germany; he was himself a German citizen, and had received his legal training in the universities of the Wilhemine Reich. Alcide De Gasperi, for his part, was born near Trentino, in the Italian lands of the Habsburg empire, studied at the University of Vienna and became a spokesman of the Catholic opposition to fascism. It is a revealing detail that during their meetings these three men spoke in German, their common language.[32] In a certain sense, it was the cosmopolitan tradition of a Germany at the margins, anti-nationalist and multicultural, that created the foundations of European unity. While Germany was freeing itself from its chauvinist past, Zionism sought to turn the page of the diaspora and 'regenerate' the Jews by nationalism, in a state whose frontiers marked a separation from a hostile surrounding world and whose laws defined citizenship on strictly religious and ethnic grounds. Eurocentric and colonial, the territorialist and statist project of Israel's founders not only aimed at separating Jews strictly from Arabs, but also drew dividing lines within their own camp, viewing eastern Jews as a kind of ersatz: substitutes for the Ashkenaze exterminated by Nazism. The condition for their integration was the negation of their history and culture, and their Westernization, in other words their assimilation to a 'superior' civilization that, in the words of Ben-Gurion, was quite contrary to 'the spirit of the Levant, which corrupts individuals and societies'.[33]

The same holds for the memory of the Holocaust. In Germany this challenged the traditional historical consciousness and promoted a reform of the nationality law that transformed the former ethnic community into a political community belonging to all its citizens, whatever their origins. In Israel, the Holocaust was used as a source of legitimation for a state reserved for Jews alone, halfway between a confessional state and an ethnic one.

In Europe, anti-Semitism ceased to be the social and cultural norm and became a deplorable anomaly, with the memory of the Shoah made into a moral pillar of our liberal democracies. By a strange metamorphosis, condemnation of the Nazi crimes against the Jews became a touchstone of morality, decency and respectability, qualities formerly denied to the Jews on the grounds of birth alone. The stigma suffered by Gershon Bleichröder, banker to Bismarck, and drawn on by Proust for his portraits of Swann and Bloch, was transformed into a mark of distinction.[34] As Régis Debray put it, with a hint of irony, 'Levinas replaced Maurras in the essays of the future high official'.[35]

The end of the twentieth century thus seems to mark the end of a historical cycle – the long history of anti-Semitism – and to change the place of Jews in European societies. The gains are incontestable (the end of social exclusion), but the losses are so as well, even if they cannot be weighed on the same scales. The end of the pariah people closes a long stage of modernity in which Jews were one of the main seedbeds of critical thought in the Western world. Today, they can still perpetuate a 'tradition', what Günther Anders called the 'tradition of anti-traditionalism',[36] but one generated by historical conditions that no longer exist. Leaving aside the few remaining champions of anti-Semitism, no one can regret this, but the exclusion and marginality of the Jews, by forcing them to think *against* – against the state, against accepted ideas, against orthodoxies and domination – stimulated a creativity and generated a critical spirit of exceptional power and scope. This phenomenon had already been noted by Tocqueville, when he emphasized the mediocrity of American democracy's cultural productions compared to the critical subtlety of men of letters under the *Ancien Régime*: 'Under the absolute government of one man, despotism, to reach the soul, crudely struck the body; and the soul, escaping from these blows, rose gloriously above it; but in democratic republics, tyranny does not proceed in this way; it leaves the body alone and goes right to the soul.'[37] This comment naturally applied to the European mind as a whole, but it was Jewish intellectuals who revealed a great tectonic shift. Once recognized and accepted, they ceased to think against the current.

According to the historian Josef H. Yerushalmi, the past century broke the myth of a 'royal alliance'. Instead of assuring protection to Jews, state power became an instrument of their persecution, and finally of their annihilation.[38] The present book takes a different approach, not seeing Jews as actors in a separate history, an endogenous process, but rather as a seismograph of the shocks that struck and transformed the modern world.[39] Its focus is Europe, the axis of the Jewish world during its phase of modernity, though also bringing into the picture the shifts to America and Israel that took place after the Second World War. Demographers predict, at least for the Jews of the Old World, a future somewhere between a slow but inexorable decline and a virtual extinction. Orthodox Jews are already a folkloric phenomenon, some observers note, in the same way as the Amish of Pennsylvania.[40] As for Jewish thought, this has ceased to be a living reality – Emmanuel Lévinas and Jacob Taubes were probably its last representatives in Europe – even if it has never been sufficiently studied in our universities. But it would be short-sighted indeed to interpret the 'Jewish question' exclusively in the light of the amputations inflicted on it by the Nazis, of its demographic decline and the ineluctable secularization of contemporary societies. Despite being secularized, it continues to exist, by forming the European past. The question asked by Gershom Scholem in February 1940, 'What will become of Europe after the elimination of the Jews?'[41] continues to haunt Europeans today, precisely because it remains unheard. That is why the 'Jewish question', in its new forms, continues to be a mirror of our culture and our democracies.

In the perspective of a conceptual history, the phrase 'Jewish question' is an ambiguous and polysemic formula.[42] It relates to the sequence described above, from 1750 to 1950, when the very existence of Jews seemed to pose a problem once the ghetto walls were abolished: for societies widely pervaded by anti-Semitic prejudice, and even for Jews themselves, forced to rethink their identity and their future outside the ghetto. The two dimensions come together in Theodor Herzl's introduction to his famous Zionist manifesto, in particular when he writes that 'the Jewish question still exists. It would be foolish to deny it.'[43] Basically, there have always been two Jewish questions. On the one hand, that which under the fascist regimes gave its name to bodies set up to destroy the conquests of emancipation. Adolf Eichmann was its leading Nazi official, Louis Darquier de Pellepoix its emblematic figure in occupied France, where he headed the sadly famous Commissariat aux questions juives. On the other hand, that of Karl Marx, Abraham Léon or Jean-Paul Sartre, authors of essays that tackle this 'question' from a different angle, that of the oppression of Jews.[44] In Europe today, this 'Jewish question' is no longer posed; in Israel, on the other hand, it has been replaced by a 'Palestinian question', itself interpreted in two ways: on the one hand, as an obstacle within the 'Jewish state', on the other, as an oppression to combat. In the Old World, the 'Jewish question' has metamorphosed into a 'place of memory', to use Pierre Nora's term: the catalogue of a piece of European history that no longer possesses 'milieus of memory' enabling it to subsist as a living reality; an inventory of which we feel the need at a time when, particularly in central and eastern Europe, its constitutive elements have ceased to exist.[45] In a Europe now pacified after a thousand-year history of conflicts and wars, Auschwitz constitutes one of the few places of shared memory,[46] inscribed in the past of almost all Europe's national segments. After its eclipse, the 'Jewish question' has become a metaphor for European history.

2
Cosmopolitanism, Mobility and Diaspora

Any reflection on Jewish modernity immediately comes up against cosmopolitanism, its key and founding dimension. A comparative approach to the transformations that affected the Jewish diaspora between 1750 and 1950, between Germany on the one hand as cradle of this modernity, and the other major centres of Jewry, in particular the tsarist empire and France, reveals its striking features.

The sons of Ahasuerus

As we have seen, Jewish existence was structured for centuries by mobility, circulation, commercial exchange, acculturation, exile and multilingualism. This explains the widespread myth of the 'wandering Jew' – marked from its origins with a strong anti-Semitic connotation: Ahasuerus, condemned to eternal vagabondage between continents and nations.[1] This figure became the metaphor of a minority living on the margins of society, partly by choice and partly by constraint.[2] Certain significant figures of modern Jewish culture, from the writer Joseph Roth to the painter Marc Chagall, illustrated this myth in their works. And a cosmopolitanism of this kind has in many respects been the fate of many Jewish intellectuals in the twentieth century, torn between tradition and modernity, between their anchorage in religious continuity and their insertion in a secularized world, or again between Europe and America, or between both continents and Israel. One need only think of Albert Einstein, who began his scientific career in Germany and ended it in Princeton. Or Chagall, who left Vitebsk for Paris, and Elias Canetti, whose literary trajectory led him to London after having lived in the Balkans, Vienna and Zurich. Or again, Isaac Bashevis Singer, the great Yiddish-language story-teller and like

Canetti a Nobel laureate for literature, who left Warsaw for New York in the mid 1930s.

Cosmopolitanism remained a structural element of the Jewish history that took shape after emancipation, when this ceased to be a separate history and became intertwined with that of the nations in which Jews lived and with which they completely identified. The great age of Jewish cosmopolitanism began in the second half of the nineteenth century, when a gigantic wave of migration drove millions of Jews from eastern Europe to the west, to Berlin and Vienna, Paris and London, finally and above all to the United States. It ended after the Second World War, when the process had been first stopped by the Nazi genocide, then channelled by the state of Israel, the destination of survivors and a centre of attraction still today for a nomadism extended over several generations. Between 1880 and the Great War, some fifteen million emigrants arrived in the United States from southern and eastern Europe, Italy and the Balkans, the Habsburg and tsarist empires. Jews made up more than 10 per cent of this enormous mass, fleeing both anti-Semitic persecution and the social dislocation of the ghetto, with intensive industrialization and urbanization threatening the old structure of Jewish small trade. In 1910, Jews made up 71.6 per cent of immigrants from the tsarist empire and more than 90 per cent of those from Romania.[3] In the east, Jewish modernity was born with the break-up of the *shtetlakh*, the traditional Jewish villages. In parallel with this, there was a massive influx to the big cities, Warsaw, Lodz, Berlin, Vienna, Prague and Budapest. Jewish cosmopolitanism thus had two main focuses: *Yiddishkeit* and *Mitteleuropa*. Here we shall focus principally on the second of these, which was a crossroads between east and west.

Mitteleuropa – the German word for central Europe[4] – was in many respects a Jewish creation. It was the Jews who cemented the unity of a cultural world that spilled over state frontiers and penetrated Slavic, Balkan and Italian culture. Germany was never for Jews a *Vaterland* of 'blood and soil', rather a language and culture that they came to interpret, renew and enrich by mingling it with other cultures and traditions. It was the German language of the Prague writer Kafka, the Bukovina poet Paul Celan, the Viennese writers Joseph Roth, Stefan Zweig, Robert Musil, Hermann Broch and Elias Canetti, who entitled the first volume of his autobiography *The Tongue Set Free*. *Yiddishkeit*, for its part, is a modern culture, born in the nineteenth-century tsarist empire that flourished in the great capitals of the Jewish diaspora, from Warsaw to Vilnius, Berlin to New York. A culture that could not live withdrawn into itself, but needed permanent contact with surrounding cultures. Its representatives travelled between one capital and another, one country and another, making Yiddish live in symbiosis with Polish, Russian, German, French and English. They often seemed suspended in the air, like the figures in Chagall's paintings, in which rabbis and cows fly above the rooftops. They were *Luftmenschen*, literally 'men of the air', with no real home of their own. They included a great number of 'rootless revolutionaries', from Trotsky to Rosa Luxemburg, who made socialism their homeland and championed a universalist spirit above national identities and borders.

German was the lingua franca of the *Mitteleuropa* Jews, not just in Berlin and Vienna but equally in Riga and Czernowitz, Prague and Budapest. True, there was a difference between Wilhelm II's Germany and multinational Austria, but it was overcome by a certain cultural homogeneity due to mobility and exchange. It was completely natural for Kafka, as a Prague author writing in German, to publish his books in Leipzig or Berlin, and for an Austrian socialist intellectual such as Rudolf Hilferding to become Germany's economics minister under the Weimar republic. Caring little for state borders, Jews shaped the cultural unity of German-speaking central Europe, in which they formed – we can say a posteriori – a 'community of fate'.[5]

Emancipation

Emancipation, cultural assimilation and the socio-economic rise of German Jews stretched across a 'long' nineteenth century. Emancipation should not be reduced simply to its legal dimension, the decrees that from the Napoleonic age through to Bismarck granted Jews German or Austrian citizenship. The term refers rather to a cumulative process spread over time, marked both by forward leaps and backward slips, but its general line was unmistakably ascendant. Moreover, 'assimilation' should not be understood as the loss of a specific cultural identity, but rather as its transformation by the generalized adoption of German language and culture.[6] The path of emancipation began in the late eighteenth century, with the reform projects of the Prussian official Wilhelm von Dohm, and was completed in 1871, with the proclamation of German unity. Its pinnacle was the constitution of the Weimar republic, drafted with the key contribution of a Jewish jurist, Hugo Preuss. Assimilation began with Moses Mendelssohn, who translated the Bible into German for Jewish readers, and culminated during the First World War with the celebration by the philosopher Hermann Cohen of a 'Judeo-German symbiosis', in an exalted patriotic spirit.[7] During this period, when the Jews of the *Kaiserreich* proudly proclaimed their Germanness, circulation and mobility were developing in the east, where starting in the 1880s a great wave of migration propelled hundreds of thousands of Jews from the tsarist empire to the United States. But the Germanization that was sought after, claimed and constantly proclaimed by a wide set of civic and cultural associations, always in the front line in patriotic celebrations, in no way stemmed the cosmopolitanism of a group whose social life and cultural identity was always defined in a European space that transcended frontiers. In other words, if Jewishness was conceived throughout the nineteenth century in a national-German form, its modalities of existence very often preserved a religious anchorage and expressed a specific demographic dynamic; they were inscribed in transnational economic networks and shared in a wide movement of European, even international, cultural transfer. This set of factors formed what we can call, in summary terms, the structural base of Jewish cosmopolitanism.

Two examples can help us understand better this coexistence of a new national identity and an old cosmopolitanism. At Versailles, in February 1871, the Franco-Prussian summit that followed the German victory put the issue of reparations on the agenda. Each of the two delegations included bankers who had greatly contributed to the financing of the war. For the French delegation there was Alphonse de Rothschild, formerly banker to the Second Empire and now in the service of Thiers; for the German delegation, Gerson Bleichröder, banker to Bismarck. Both came originally from Frankfurt. Gerson's father, Samuel Bleichröder, had been sent to Berlin in 1828 by the Rothschild house in Frankfurt, as also had James (Jacob) Rothschild, the father of Alphonse.[8] Despite subsequently belonging to two different national entities, they issued from one and the same tradition, that of the 'court Jews' or *Hofjuden* who for centuries had been a major factor in the economic development of Europe under the *Ancien Régime*.[9]

The Franco-Prussian war was also the object of impassioned and tense correspondence between German Jews living either side of the Rhine. Abraham Geiger and Joseph Darmsteter were long-standing friends since the time that they studied together at the University of Bonn and followed the neo-orthodox teaching of Samson-Raphaël Hirsch. Geiger settled in Berlin, where he taught Jewish philosophy and theology at the school of the 'science of Judaism'; Darmsteter migrated to France, where he made a brilliant career as historian and geographer at the École pratique des hautes études. The rise of nationalisms in Europe divided them, the former becoming a German patriot, the latter a French one. The correspondence between Geiger and Darmsteter, just like the confrontation between Rothschild and Bleichröder, thus revealed a split that had occurred within German Jewry in the course of the nineteenth century: on the one hand, a structural cosmopolitanism, on the other hand, new constraints arising from an emancipation effected within a national state.[10]

The final phase in the history of German Jewry, on the other hand, from the end of the First World War to the advent of Nazism, was characterized by the explicit claim of cosmopolitanism. It saw the rise of a new intellectual generation that viewed assimilation as an accomplished fact, we could almost say an existential datum, rather than a goal to attain, but that also was faced with the rise of a violent anti-Semitism, no longer religious but racial.[11] This Jewish cosmopolitanism, in the majority of cases largely secularized, was a response to the crisis of the emancipation process whose gains, especially from 1930, proved to be increasingly fragile and precarious. Between 1933 and 1938, this intellectual cosmopolitanism gave way to one no longer chosen but forced, that of a community expelled from Germany as a foreign body. Destroyed in Europe, Jewish-German culture pursued its path in exile.

Cultural transfers

The nineteenth century was an age of great migratory movements. Tens of thousands of Jews left their *shtetalkh*, the Jewish villages of central and eastern Europe, to settle in town, especially in the capital cities of the Habsburg and Wilhelmine empires. It was in the context of this multiform upheaval – the demographic growth and the urbanization process generated by the industrial revolution, modernization and assimilation – that German Jewry acquired a new profile. Vienna, where no more than 2,000 Jews had lived in 1850, counted more than 200,000 on the eve of the First World War, or 10 per cent of the total population; in the same timeframe, the Jewish population of Berlin grew from less than 10,000 to nearly 200,000, here making up 7 per cent of the total population.[12] The Jewish populations of Budapest, Prague, Lvov, Krakow and Czernowitz underwent similar growth. These cities absorbed Jewish immigrants from the eastern regions of the Prussian empire (Silesia, Poznan) and the Slavic regions of the Habsburg empire (Galicia, Bukovina, Moravia, Slovakia, Bohemia). This intensive urbanization was accompanied by a secularization of lifestyles and, above all, a cultural assimilation that led to the gradual abandonment of Yiddish in favour of German. Vienna and Berlin likewise contained districts of immigrants from the tsarist empire, Russians and Poles, who preserved their community life until becoming centres of diffusion of Jewish modernism in the 1920s.

In the space of two generations, Jews became a relatively well-off community, belonging mainly to the middle class and sharing fully in the different strata of the educated bourgeoisie (*Bildungsbürgertum*).[13] Then, under the impulse of their elites (reformed and liberal), a strategy of 'confessionalization' was put in place. Jews saw themselves as German citizens of 'Judaic faith' (*deutsche Staatsbürger jüdischen Glaubens*), alongside Catholics and Protestants. Excluded de facto from public function – there were practically no Jews in the civil service and the military hierarchy, and very few in the university faculties – they found in culture a privileged path of assertion and recognition. It was *Bildung*, an expression that indicates a set of values – education, good behaviour, accomplishment, moral concern, manners – that enabled them to feel completely Germans.[14] Perceived by the majority of their compatriots of 'German stock' as a body foreign to the nation, they were citizens of the Reich but not members of the German *Volk*, whose boundaries, though invisible, remained solid, not to say unbreachable.

It may be useful, in order to focus the profile of this community, to compare it with its neighbours, the Russian and Polish *Ostjuden*, as well as those of the west, in particular France. In Russia, given a state anti-Semitism that perpetuated old forms of exclusion and persecution, Jewish modernity acquired a national character focused on the renewal of Yiddish language and culture. In France, where emancipation went back to 1791, this was the motor of cultural assimilation rather than the cultural dimension either replacing or preceding the political. Under the Third Republic, a broad stratum of 'state Jews' prospered: top officials, army officers, university professors and ministers.[15] In Italy a similar process developed extremely rapidly in the second half of the nineteenth century, in the wake of national unification. In these two countries, accordingly, anti-Semitism was either anti-modern (Italian Catholicism) or 'subversive' (French nationalism), attacking institutions perceived as Jewish creations, 'infiltrated' and 'corrupted' from within.[16] Unlike Treitschke's Germany, it did not seek to preserve the ethnic and Christian character of the state. Midway between tsarist Russia and republican France, Jewish identity in Germany was constructed on the cultural axis of *Bildung* rather than the national one of *Yiddishkeit* or a political one (citizenship as matrix of the nation). Whereas a Russian or Polish Jew was not Russian or Polish, but a Jewish subject of the tsarist empire, and a French Israelite was a full citizen of republican France (anti-Semitic hostility being directed precisely against the republic), a German Jew remained, despite his assimilation, the member of an ethno-cultural minority widely perceived as 'non-German'. Norbert Elias has given a very accurate definition of this condition: 'It is a singular experience to belong to a stigmatized minority while at the same time being wholly embedded in the cultural flow and the political and social fate of the stigmatizing majority.'[17] This feeling of exclusion and non-belonging acquired a quite paradoxical character at the turn of the century, when Jews gained a leading place in cultural life, leading Moritz Goldstein to write: 'We Jews manage the intellectual inheritance of a people that grants us neither the right nor the capacity to do so.'[18]

Keeping in mind these different models of construction of Jewish modernity aids a better understanding of the contradictory, and sometimes diametrically opposite, effects of the diffusion and radiation of German-Jewish culture in the rest of Europe. Two examples of cultural transfer serve to illustrate this phenomenon: the spread of *Haskalah* in eastern Europe and the metamorphoses of the *Wissenschaft des Judentums* in France.

Haskalah, the Jewish Enlightenment in late eighteenth-century Germany given its initial impulse by Moses Mendelssohn, prepared the ground for the legislation on emancipation. In other words, *Haskalah* appears in hindsight as the first stage in the construction of a modern German-Jewish identity, assimilated and secularized.[19] In the tsarist empire, on the other hand, where its impact was only felt much later, in the late nineteenth century, it led not to assimilation, but to the modernization and secularization of a Jewish identity that saw itself as distinctly national.[20] In a context dominated by anti-Semitism – championed by the state and deeply rooted in society – the opening of the Jewish world to the major currents of Western modernity took the form of a renewal of Yiddish culture, the foundation of a Jewish nation in the diaspora. As Régine Robin points out, this is a fascinating paradox if we consider the bitter struggle waged by the German *Haskalah* against Yiddish, the jargon of the ghetto and emblem of a culture denounced as irredeemably obscurantist.[21]

The key organizational expression of German Judaism's assimilation strategy was the Zentralverein deutscher Staatsbürger jüdischen Glaubens (central association of German citizens of Jewish faith), patriotic and liberal in orientation, whose intellectual support was a still older institution, the 'science of Judaism' (*Wissenschaft des Judentums*) school.[22] Founded in 1819 in Berlin by Eduard Gans and Leopold Zunz, this school was a kind of Jewish university, differing from rabbinical seminars in being open to a secular public, and with all its teaching in German. It lay at the origin of a new interpretation of Judaism destined to exert a wide influence right across Europe. Radically opposed to the mystical and messianic tendencies, it proceeded to a rationalist interpretation of Judaism. Theology was subjected to a rigorous exegesis of texts, conducted with the aid of philology, while Jewish history began to be studied according to scientific criteria – verification of sources, systematic use of archives – under the aegis of Heinrich Graetz.[23] The school of the 'science of Judaism', born from the *Haskalah*, sought to inscribe Jewish history in the broader context of German and European history.

In this German context, however, the *Wissenschaft des Judentums* could act as a vehicle for the preservation of Judaism by its modernization. Exported to France, in an 'Israelite' community largely of German origin, this school underwent a completely different trajectory, contributing in the end to the dissolution of a specifically Jewish culture and thought. As Perrine Simon-Nahum has brilliantly shown in *La cité investie*, Israelite scholars educated in this school did not build a Jewish cultural and scientific institution but finished their careers in the French republic's most prestigious academic institutions. The philologist Solomon Munk took over from Ernest Renan at the Collège de France, the historian Joseph Derenbourg joined the École pratique des hautes études and a specialist in the Kabbalah, Adolphe Frank, became a member of the Institut Français. These different trajectories out of a common matrix gave rise to two classic and diametrically opposite works: Julius Guttmann's *Die Philosophie des Judentums* (1933) and Émile Durkheim's *Elementary Forms of Religious Life* (1912), a foundational study of modern sociology, whose scientific approach presupposes a completely secularized worldview.[24] Whereas Guttmann's book follows in the lineage of the 'science of Judaism', Durkheim's broke completely with that tradition.

Exclusion

Lying behind this German-Jewish model of cultural assimilation combined with political exclusion was a more pronounced rift within German *Bildungsbürgertum*, that between Jews and non-Jews. The former identified the normative ideal of *Bildung* with the Enlightenment, giving it a universalist interpretation; the latter tended to re-inscribe Enlightenment values in an increasingly tight national mould. Assimilation enabled Jews to appropriate German culture, but the stigmatization affecting them – despite their socio-economic and cultural success – deprived them in the public sphere of the attributes of morality, dignity and respectability, the 'ethicalness' (*Sittlichkeit*) that remained an exclusive privilege of 'Aryan' Germans. In brief, German Jews were prisoners of what George L. Mosse analysed as an insurmountable contradiction between *Bildung* and *Sittlichkeit*, the former being increasingly Judaized, while the latter remained ever unattainable, even by individuals as rich and powerful as the banker Gerson Bleichröder or the industrialist Walther Rathenau.[25] It was in this context that anti-Semitism fulfilled its function as a cultural code necessary to the definition of a problematic German identity. The cult of ancestral and aristocratic Germany was opposed to (Jewish) modernity, and German identity was negatively defined by opposition to Judaism.[26]

The identification of Jews with cosmopolitanism was a war-cry of anti-Semitism, from Treitschke to Hitler. Jews became an indispensable element in the opposition between *Kultur* and *Zivilisation* that almost perfectly mirrored the dichotomy between Germanness and Jewishness. The Jew embodied the mobility of money and finance, cosmopolitanism and abstract universalism, international law and 'degenerate' urban culture. The German, on the other hand, was rooted in the land, created wealth by work and not by financial operations, possessed a culture that expressed a national spirit, did not view the borders of his state as abstract legal constructions but as the markers of a *Lebensraum*: these dogmas were repeated by dozens of authors from the foundation of the Wilhelmian reich onwards. Their traces are very visible in the writings of the geographers Friedrich Ratzel and Karl Haushofer, the economist Werner Sombart, the political philosopher Carl Schmitt, the writer Ernst Jünger, the philosopher Oswald Spengler, the pan-Germanist Arthur Möller van den Bruck, the literary critic Paul de Lagarde, the racist theorist Houston Stewart Chamberlain and many others. A significant common characteristic of these anti-Semitic texts was their metaphorical use of the figure of the Jew, required for a valuation of German nationalism through its opposition to Jewish cosmopolitanism.

This anti-Semitism spurred Jewish writers to look abroad for a recognition denied them in their homeland. This created a paradox: German literature was represented in Europe by Jewish writers rejected as foreigners in their own country. In an essay on Stefan Zweig, Hannah Arendt defined the cosmopolitanism of German-Jewish writers as 'a marvellous nationality that they claimed when reminded of their Jewish origin, which somewhat resembles those modern passports that grant the bearer the right of sojourn in every country expect the one that issued it'.[27]

In 1933, exiled in Paris, Joseph Roth emphasized the 'natural tendency towards cosmopolitanism' of Jewish men of letters:

> The indisputable contribution of Jewish writers to German letters lies in the discovery and literary valorization of urbanism. Jews discovered and illustrated the urban landscape and the mental

landscape of town-dwellers. They revealed the many faces of urban civilization. They showed the café and the factory, the bar and the hotel, the bank and the petty bourgeoisie of the capital, the meeting places of the rich and the wretched districts of the poor, the sins and vices, the city of day and the city of night, the character of the inhabitants of the great metropolises. This orientation of Jewish talent arose from the urban milieu that the majority of them came from, a milieu to which their parents had been attracted for economic reasons; it also arose from their more developed sensibility and the natural tendency of Jews to cosmopolitanism [*kosmopolitische Begabung*]. The majority of non-Jewish German writers confined themselves to describing the rural landscape that was their home. There exists in Germany, to a greater degree than anywhere else, a 'homeland literature' [*Heimatliteratur*] devoted to the regions, the countryside and the villages, sometimes of a high literary level, but by necessity inaccessible to fellow-Europeans. Abroad there was only one 'Germany', its literary interpreters being in the majority Jewish writers.[28]

Consequently, Roth added, they were all the more detested in their own country, criticized for their 'distance from the land', denounced as *Kaffeehausliteraten* and often even as 'traitors to the fatherland'.

Internationalism

This contradiction between *Bildung* and *Sittlichkeit*, assimilation and anti-Semitism, could give rise to a radical form of cosmopolitanism that equally rejected German nationalism and Judaism; in other words, a quest for identity of a post-national type. This phenomenon appeared early on, in the time of emancipation, with Ludwig Börne, Moses Hess and Karl Marx, broadening out in the early twentieth century with the rise of the socialist and communist movement. A controversial text such as *Zur Judenfrage*, written by the young Marx in 1843, is a relatively faithful mirror of this new form of universalist thought.[29] Often anachronistically interpreted as a sign of 'self-hatred' on the part of the young Marx, what it is really is a plea for a 'universal human emancipation' that inevitably has to go beyond the boundaries of Judaism. Viewing the latter as a form of religious obscurantism, and interpreting it as a metaphor for modern capitalism, the text expresses an orientation that was quite common among young Jewish intellectuals in the 1840s, prisoners of a double contradiction: on the one hand, the impossibility of returning to traditional Judaism on account of their assimilation, and on the other hand, the impossibility of fully acceding to Germanity on account of the surrounding anti-Semitism. They chose to reject both, superseding them in a cosmopolitan perspective.[30]

From this point of view, Marx was simply a precursor. At the turn of the century, socialism was a privileged expression of Jewish cosmopolitanism, as shown at the time by Robert Michels in his famous study on the sociology of political parties. Michel indicated the massive presence of Jewish intellectuals in the upper ranks of German social-democracy, giving this a double explanation: on the one hand, the resentment arising from the crying 'inequality of treatment' they were subjected to in German society; on the other hand, 'the cosmopolitan tendency which has been highly developed in the Jews by the historical experiences of the race'.[31]

It was Germany that attracted figures such as Rosa Luxemburg, Alexander Israel Helphand (Parvus) and Karl Radek, who profoundly marked the modern definition of internationalism. They drew its contours both theoretically (the analysis of capitalism as a world system, the theory of permanent revolution) and practically (opposition to the wave of nationalism that took hold of Europe in 1914), playing a fundamental role in the transformation of Enlightenment universalism into socialist internationalism. It was in Germany, both because of its crucial geographical position at the heart of Europe and because of its singular cultural position, halfway between nation-state and multinational empire, between Jewish assimilation and Yiddish national renaissance, that Jews became the actors of this metamorphosis. In a certain sense, Jewish cosmopolitanism was a substratum of internationalism.

Until the Russian Revolution, Jewish internationalism was focused above all in the Yiddish-speaking world. The Bund, founded in 1897, established itself not just in Vilnius and Warsaw but also in New York, which had five Yiddish daily papers in the early twentieth century; *Forverts*, of socialist orientation, had the largest circulation with a print run of 175,000 copies.[32] The Bund both preceded and stimulated the birth of Russian (or more accurately, pan-Russian) social-democracy, in which Jewish intellectuals were well represented in all of its currents, from Mensheviks (Julius Martov, Fyodor Dan) to Bolsheviks (Lev Kamenev, Gregory Zinoviev). After the Russian Revolution, they were among the leading lights in the Communist International, of which Zinoviev was first secretary. Jewish intellectuals were at the head of the revolutions that overthrew the central empires and led, as in Bavaria and Hungary, to ephemeral soviet-type republics in 1919. We need only mention Rosa Luxemburg, Leo Jogiches and Paul Levi in Berlin; Kurt Eisner, Gustav Landauer, Ernst Toller and Eugen Leviné in Munich; Bela Kun and Georg Lukács in Budapest; Otto Bauer, Max and Friedrich Adler in Vienna.[33]

Liberalism had been discredited, the peace and prosperity of the nineteenth century had disappeared on the battlefields of the Great War, while conservative and nationalist parties did not admit Jews to their ranks. This context left only one alternative for young Jewish intellectuals: either adhesion to Zionism, their own version of nationalism, or to socialism and communism, whose internationalist aims were interpreted as the assertion of a European and universalist identity against the rise of nationalisms.[34] Some people discovered, in the wake of Martin Buber, Jewish identity and the nationalism of 'blood' (even if it would be wrong to classify Buber in the category of racism, as in his writing this notion has an essentially spiritual and metaphorical connotation). The internationalism of others was often forgetful of the Jewish 'little difference', and could even be hostile to this. In 1917, Rosa Luxemburg, interned in a Prussian prison on account of her opposition to the war, expressed this universalism now foreign to Jewishness in almost poetic terms. In relation to the miseries of the world, she wrote to her friend Mathilde Wurm, there was no 'special place' left in her heart for the suffering of the Jews: 'I feel at home in the entire world, wherever there are clouds and birds and tears.'[35]

German Jewry entered its final phase in the 1930s, before finding a tragic epilogue in the Nazi death camps. Cosmopolitanism had become an obligatory motto when, under the Weimar republic, the nationalists insulted all newspapers that defended democracy, from *Die Weltbühne* to the *Frankfurter Zeitung*, as the '*Judenpresse*'. Peter Gay described Weimar culture as a kind of 'dance on the edge of an abyss', led by 'outsiders as insiders' for whom exile became their 'true home'.[36]

Between 1933 and 1938, a great exodus of German Jews began, far greater in its extent than that of the Spanish Jews after 1492 or that of the Huguenots after the revocation of the edict of Nantes. More than 450,000 Jews left central Europe as it came under Nazi rule.[37] The whole of German-Jewish culture was exiled, establishing new capitals first in Paris, and then from 1940 in New York.[38] This uprooting would be definitive, as the great majority of exiles did not return to Germany after the war and the Shoah. The refugees saw themselves charged with the mission of perpetuating the tradition of *Aufklärung* that Nazism sought to destroy. They founded German-language papers and reviews, and even publishing houses that survived despite enormous material difficulties. The spirit in which they worked is well illustrated by a small book by Walter Benjamin published in Switzerland in 1934 under the title of *Deutsche Menschen*.[39] Benjamin presented this anthology, for which he had collected letters of philosophers and writers from the age of Enlightenment, as 'an ark built on a Jewish model', its aim being to rescue German culture from the flood that threatened to drown it.[40] This mission of preservation and rescue was accompanied among many exiles with an acute awareness of their Jewishness, identified not by a religion but by cosmopolitanism. It was thus that Siegfried Kracauer wrote in 1938 a biography of Jacques Offenbach, the German-Jewish composer exiled in France under the Second Empire, whose 'extra-territoriality' he celebrated, a notion in which it is not hard to read, in relief, the fate of German Jews in the twentieth century.[41] Stefan Zweig's autobiography has the subtitle 'memories of a European', well indicating the transnational dimension of his experience as a Viennese writer rather than simply as an Austrian.[42] And Joseph Roth explicitly presented himself as lacking a homeland, a citizen of the world (*Weltbürger*) and even, with a touch of irony that is not altogether inexact, a *Hotelpatriot*.[43]

The German-Jewish exile of the 1930s lay at the root of a cultural transfer of very wide scope. American culture was deeply and lastingly transformed by this 'graft'. The scientific pre-eminence acquired by the great American universities after the Second World War owed much to the contribution of these exiles from central Europe.[44] The role that they played in the Manhattan Project, thanks to which the United States became the first nuclear power, was an emblematic illustration of a far wider phenomenon touching on historiography and philosophy, psychoanalysis and sociology, film and music, etc. Some historians have even spoken in this respect of a shift in the world's axis from one side of the Atlantic to the other.[45]

The Americanization of German Jews involved the discovery of a republican political culture – based on the valuation of law and individual freedom – that was always marginal in Germany, where political exclusion was the corollary of intellectual excellence. Educated in the school of *Bildung*, German intellectuals discovered in the United States the Bill of Rights.[46] A good part of American political science – starting with the theory of totalitarianism, developed in the 1940s by Hans Kohn, Franz Neumann and Hannah Arendt – was the product of this encounter, involving a mutation both in the culture of origin and in that of the country of reception, in a manner analysed by the exiled sociologist Karl Mannheim.[47] Adopted in the nineteenth century as a strategy of assimilation, *Bildung* almost constituted an obstacle to the integration of Jews in an American society that, after challenging the old 'Wasp' paradigm under the impact of European integration, now recognized itself as ethnically and culturally plural. America had been the haven for German-Jewish cosmopolitanism. And it was the place where this odyssey came to an end.

3
Intellectuals Between Critique and Power

Within the intellectual world, the end of Jewish modernity took the form of a conservative turn. In order to distinguish the stages of this process, it is essential to look back at the golden age (1750–1950). It is by comparison between the first and second halves of the twentieth century, separated by the caesura of war and Holocaust, that the full scope of this turn becomes apparent. The change that took place at this time affected the very status of the Jewish intellectual, a status that we shall seek in this chapter to locate in its proper historical perspective.

'Mercurians' and 'non-Jewish Jews'

In an essay of his youth that has become both famous and controversial, Karl Marx presented Judaism as a source of modernity, and capitalism as the result of a 'Judaized' world.[1] This is also in broad lines the thesis of the American historian of Russian-Jewish origin, Yuri Slezkine. In his eyes, the modernization of the world coincides with its Judaization, on condition that Jews are not defined – or not solely defined – as a religious community, but rather as a minority historically constituted around certain major characteristics that today are universally shared: market, communication, mobility, the bridging of languages and cultures, intellectual specialization. Jews embodied the market economy from the Middle Ages on, and managed the affairs of European courts long before the advent of finance capitalism. They experienced exile and learned to live in a diaspora several centuries before the concept of 'globalization' appeared in our vocabulary. Commerce, banking, law, textual interpretation and cultural mediation always organized their existence. Emancipation propelled them to the centre of modernity, as an elite of 'Mercurians' (foreign and mobile, producers of concepts) in a world of 'Apollonians' (sedentary warriors, producers of goods).² In short, Slezkine constructs a metaphor of Jewish history by emphasizing the organic link connecting it to the modern world. But not only did Jews prefigure capitalist globalization, they were also its sharpest critics, inspiring and sometimes leading the majority of revolutionary movements, both intellectual and political, of the last two centuries. They embodied modernity in its different dimensions, being at the same time its precursors, actors, critics and victims: if the twentieth century was the 'Jewish century', it was also the culminating moment of anti-Semitism.

As we have seen, it was especially in central and eastern Europe, where they formed large minorities before the Second World War, that Jews lived as 'foreign' and 'marginal'. Emancipation led in a short space of time to the dissolution of the old religious community withdrawn into itself, by promoting an extraordinary wave of modernization and cultural assimilation. Emerging from the synagogue and separated from their tradition despite remaining 'foreigners' in an often hostile world, Jews embodied an 'alterity' that, if complex, varied and thus hard to define, was clearly perceptible. On the one hand, they embraced the cause of 'progress'; on the other, they were the privileged target of conservative culture. The rising new nationalisms saw Jewish cosmopolitanism as their natural enemy. From the *Berlinerstreit* to the Dreyfus affair, from Treitschke to Drumont and Maurras, Jews were stigmatized as the representatives of a corrupting and 'degenerate' modernity. Suspended between a lost tradition and a respectability denied, they became heretics.

The notion of the 'non-Jewish Jew', formulated by Isaac Deutscher in 1958 to outline the profile of the intellectual who breaks with his inherited religion and culture, has now become a metaphor for Jewish modernity. The most striking passage in his essay, very often quoted, reads as follows:

> The Jewish heretic who transcends Jewry belongs to a Jewish tradition. You may, if you like, view Akher as a prototype of those great revolutionaries of modern thought... if you necessarily wish to place them within any Jewish tradition. They all went beyond the boundaries of Jewry. They all – Spinoza, Heine, Marx, Rosa Luxemburg, Trotsky, and Freud – found Jewry too narrow, too archaic, and too constricting. They all looked for ideals and

fulfilment beyond it, and they represent the sum and substance of much that is greatest in modern thought, the sum and substance of the most profound upheavals that have taken place in philosophy, sociology, economics, and politics in the last three centuries.[3]

It is this 'heresy' that, according to Deutscher, attaches the 'non-Jewish Jew' to Jewish tradition, drawing a line of continuity that can include both secularization and atheism.[4] As he sees it, the extraordinary explosion of intellectual creativity that characterized the Jewish world from the nineteenth century and of which the thinkers mentioned above were – among many others – the emblematic embodiment, has deep historical roots. Instead of investigating an ethnic or religious particularism, Deutscher prefers to single out two constitutive elements of Jewish modernity: cosmopolitanism and anti-conformism, in other words the life of diaspora and the status of outsider arising from social exclusion. On the one hand, Jewish intellectuals lived at the crossroads of several languages and national cultures; on the other hand, they 'were extremely vulnerable', as their unstable and fluctuating social position exposed them, as a kind of privileged scapegoat, to any form of national prejudice:

'Whenever intolerance or nationalist emotion was on the ascendant, whenever dogmatic narrow-mindedness and fanaticism triumphed, they were the first victims.' As Deutscher spells out, they were excommunicated by Jewish rabbis, expelled from their own political parties and persecuted by political authorities: 'Nearly all of them were exiled from their countries; and the writings of all were burned at the stake at one time or another.'[5]

Deutscher had known the multinational Habsburg empire and the precarious order of Europe between the two wars, the traditional Jewish world and Marxist atheism, Soviet communism and Atlantic liberalism. He studied in Krakow in the 1920s, in a Poland that had arisen from the collapse of three empires. Author of works in Polish, Yiddish and English, yet full also of Russian and German literary references, he well embodied the archetype of the central European Jewish intellectual of the first half of the twentieth century, living, in his own words, 'on the borderlines of various civilizations, religions, and national cultures'.[6] His intellectual and political itinerary was marked by two major ruptures: the first with the synagogue, the second with the communist 'church' – making him a heretic par excellence (to both Judaism and Marxism). His identification with Spinoza, Marx and Trotsky can easily be read between the lines of his essay. After the model of Rosa Luxemburg, for whom Judaism was simply a concentrate of archaic prejudices – drawn to the 'entire world', she no longer had in her heart any 'special place' for the ghetto –,[7] Deutscher was aware of having 'grown up in the past of the Jewish people', with the Jewish Middle Ages that still lived 'under his own roof'. He wanted to free himself of this inheritance, perceiving it as an obstacle to the appropriation of modern culture, and remained completely insensitive to the Hassidic Judaism that fascinated certain elements of the assimilated German-Jewish intelligentsia. 'The fashionable longing of the Western Jew for a return to the sixteenth century', he wrote, alluding to Martin Buber, had 'something unreal and Kafkaeque' about it, like an incomprehensible form of romantic mysticism.[8]

Deutscher's hero, therefore, was Spinoza. The Amsterdam philosopher, from a Marrano background, developed his thought in a particular context, marked by the clash between the Iberian inquisition and multi-confessional Holland – a situation somewhat reminiscent of that between tsarist Russia and the Habsburg empire. An intellectual outcast in a society where it was inconceivable not to belong to a religious community, Spinoza championed a philosophy of immanence that superseded Christianity as much as Judaism. In his eyes, salvation did not lie with God, but in human action in harmony with the laws of reason and nature. Accused of heresy, this champion of the radical Enlightenment was inevitably banned from the Jewish community. In his essay, Deutscher juxtaposes Spinoza to Marx, who in his controversial text of 1843 postulated a universalist ideal of human emancipation that transcended the rights and claims of particular nations.[9]

Social marginality, cosmopolitanism and national non-belonging, atheism and political anti-conformism: those were the four qualities of the 'non-Jewish Jew'. The implosion of the traditional Jewish world and the rise of modern anti-Semitism were its premises, implying a double transcendence: on the one hand, the superseding of Judaism, made necessary by the radical cleavage dividing the Jewish tradition from modernity; on the other hand, the superseding of national identities and cultures that rejected Jewish alterity. In short, the 'non-Jewish Jew' had left his community of origin, but remained excluded from the surrounding society. He became the spokesperson of a kind of post-national cosmopolitanism.

Defined in this way, the 'non-Jewish Jew' could not be identified with the champions of a modernization in national and secular forms, in the options supported at this time by Haïm Jitlowski, Simon Dubnov or Vladimir Medem, the theorists of national cultural autonomy. True, these championed a resolutely secular conception of Jewishness, but they sought to re-establish this on national foundations, no longer religious but linguistic and cultural. Deutscher, however, never hid his scepticism towards Yiddish culture, which remained in his eyes peripheral and minor. As an intransigent internationalist, he did not seek to modernize the Jewish world but to transcend it.

The 'Jewish tradition' to which he referred in his essay consisted in a heretical transcendence that was born in the seventeenth century with Spinoza, renewed in the nineteenth century by Marx and Heine, and went on to irrigate every avant-garde current of European culture in the twentieth. Basically, this tradition lay in the Jew's self-awareness of himself as outsider. Deutscher explained this in the following words:

> Religion? I am an atheist. Jewish nationalism? I am an internationalist. In neither sense am I, therefore, a Jew. I am, however, a Jew by force of my unconditional solidarity with the persecuted and exterminated. I am a Jew because I feel the Jewish tragedy as my own tragedy; because I feel the pulse of Jewish history...[10]

This portrait of the 'non-Jewish Jew' presents several affinities with other metaphorical figures of Jewish modernity. We could include it in a long gallery, alongside Georg Simmel's 'foreigner' (*Fremde*) and Hannah Arendt's 'Jewish pariah', representing a humanism arising from the lack of rights, from non-belonging and political exclusion.[11] Without being synonymous, these various concepts share the same attempt to grasp the Jewish condition between a voluntary rejection of the past and the rejection experienced from European societies prey to nationalism.

Deutscher's essay, in this heretical, cosmopolitan and revolutionary tradition, indicates the only encounter possible between Jews and modernity. Written under the impact of the Holocaust, it seems to seal the defeat of the German-Jewish symbiosis, based on an emancipation that proved illusory. Deutscher mentions at one point Moses Mendelssohn as the conceiver of a 'German-Jewish ideal [that] was of a piece with the paltry liberalism of the gentile German bourgeoisie', inwardly liberal but outwardly submissive to the Prussian regime.¹² In 1958, when de-Stalinization aroused the illusion of a possible internal reform of the Soviet system, Deutscher reasserted the Marxist postulate of a dissolution of Jewry in an emancipated society freed from every religious or racial oppression. Perhaps under the influence of Sartre's famous text published a dozen years earlier, he saw anti-Semitism as the underlying cause of the persistence of Jews in history. The 'non-Jewish Jew', who remained Jewish despite his break with Judaism, is in a certain sense constituted as a Jew by the gaze of the anti-Semite.¹³ Jews would no longer exist as a distinct community, Deutscher wrote, 'if anti-Semitism had not proved so terribly deep-rooted, persistent, and powerful in Christian-European civilization'.¹⁴

Avant-garde

If Jewish modernity began at the turn of the nineteenth century, and ended in the Nazi death camps, its premises date from well before the French Revolution. According to Daniel Lindenberg, they go back to the arrival of Spanish and Portuguese Marranos in several cities on the Mediterranean and in northern France, in Venice and Amsterdam, in the mid seventeenth century, in a Europe that had been turned upside down by the Thirty Years War and the revolution in England.¹⁵ Who were the Marranos? In the words of the historian Carl Gebhardt, 'the Marrano is a Catholic without faith and a Jew without culture, but Jewish all the same by choice'.¹⁶ In Spain in the age of the *Reconquista*, converted Jews secretly perpetuated their old religion, braving the ban on any non-Catholic cult. In Amsterdam, as well as in Hamburg and Livorno, émigré Marranos could return to Judaism, but they encountered the hostility of the rabbinical authorities, who viewed them with distrust and did not consider them as authentic Jews. Their Judaism was existential, and they were faced with a community dominated by norms, its existence fixed on the levels of doctrine and ritual. Calvinist Holland saw them as Jews, while Jews saw them as Christians. They studied Hebrew, spoke Spanish or Portuguese, wrote in Latin and lived in a cosmopolitan world. They saw Judaism not as a closed world but rather as a laboratory and a crossroads of experiences. Out of this background, Spinoza elaborated a philosophy of immanence that went beyond both Judaism and Christianity. Inevitably, this champion of the Enlightenment was accused of heresy and banished from the Jewish community.[17] The messianic hope was then rethought in a secular perspective of political emancipation (Menasseh ben Israel), reformulated as subversive apostasy (Sabbati Tsvi) or as a 'messianism of reason' (Spinoza).[18] These were in a sense the first 'non-Jewish Jews'.

These precursors heralded the great turning-point of the nineteenth century, when emancipation allowed the Jews to enter the culture of European nations. Their former 'ecological' isolation – spatial, cultural, religious and linguistic – formed what Jacob Katz sees as an almost insurmountable obstacle to their participation in the life and culture of the societies around them.[19] Once the ghetto walls were broken down, the emancipated Jews penetrated the culture of the various European countries and in two or three generations attained leading positions in almost every field, from the natural sciences to the humanities, sometimes contributing to the creation of new disciplines. German-speaking central Europe (and to a lesser degree both the Russian empire and France) was the epicentre of this creative explosion. Marcel Proust, Franz Kafka and Robert Musil renewed literature. Sigmund Freud, by inventing psychoanalysis, brought to light the hidden face of the bourgeois world, while Marc Chagall gave pictorial form to the oneiric fantasies of a continent being radically transformed. In the wake of Marx, Rosa Luxemburg, Parvus and Trotsky transformed the universalism of the Enlightenment into socialist internationalism, giving it both a theoretical form (the view of capitalism as a world system, permanent revolution) and a practical one (opposition to the First World War). Georg Simmel, Karl Mannheim, Émile Durkheim and Marcel Mauss explored modernity and described its symbols, sites and figures, from money to the city, the foreigner and the intellectual, completing the transition from religion to science. They were no longer interested in Judaism, but in the social and anthropological structures of religious life. Albert Einstein developed his theory of relativity by breaking with Newtonian physics, and Arnold Schönberg created serialism, a new atonal music, by breaking with traditional harmonies. Aby Warburg, Rudolf Arnheim and Siegfried Kracauer theorized the heuristic potential of images and deciphered the language of cinema. Theodor W. Adorno, Max Horkheimer and Herbert Marcuse grasped the destructive potentialities of instrumental rationality, focusing a critical gaze on the trajectory of Western civilization. Walter Benjamin realized the encounter between the aesthetic avant-garde and romanticism, between Jewish messianism and atheistic communism, developing a new concept of history. Hannah Arendt studied the contradictions of the system of nation-states, the birth of racism, imperialism and modern anti-Semitism, through to the rise of totalitarianisms. Ernst Bloch inventoried the utopias that have haunted the Western world since the Renaissance. Even structuralism, which flourished in Paris in the 1950s, had its beginnings in the 1941 encounter between Claude Lévi-Strauss and the linguist Roman Jakobson in New York, where the French anthropologist had fled to escape the Vichy regime's racial laws. This extraordinary explosion of creativity, which everywhere placed Jews in the midst of revolutionary movements and avant-garde currents, was followed by the permanent shadow of exclusion. From the late nineteenth century, the exacerbation of anti-Semitism rendered the Jewish intelligentsia still more sensitive to the critique of conservatism and the challenge to established powers.

'State Jews', scholars and intellectuals

We have so far considered two models of Jewish modernity in Europe: the eastern model of pariah Judaism (made up of social and political exclusion) and the German model (made up of socio-economic integration, cultural assimilation and political exclusion, despite the emancipatory laws). There is however also a third model, which we can refer to as western, based on a double recognition, both social and political, though inhibited by the presence of a lively anti-Semitism, particularly in France. Its origin lay with the 'state Jews', an elite almost absent in Germany or Austria, but particularly flourishing in Britain, France and Italy. Under the Third Republic, hundreds of Jews reached the summits of French public service: prefects, generals, state counsellors, deputies, senators and ministers, not to mention a large number of scholars and scientists admitted to the most prestigious cultural institutions such as the Collège de France.[20] By imposing a notion of citizenship incompatible with any particularism, the French republic encouraged the total identification of Jews with the nation and its institutions, which, on account of their secular character and meritocratic principle, favoured the creation of a political and administrative elite of Jewish origin. In opposition to this, the anti-republican reaction, racist and clerical, acquired a strong anti-Semitic tinge. From the Dreyfus affair to Vichy, French nationalism never stopped denouncing the 'Jewish republic'.[21]

The defining feature of French Judaism, in fact, has always been its attachment to republican institutions. Its intellectuals were Dreyfusards at the end of the nineteenth century, then nationalists in 1914, and many joined the Resistance during the Second World War. By identifying with the Third Republic, they showed evidence of a certain political conformism and, at the same time, unhesitatingly located themselves in the camp of 'progress'. The more audacious of their number proclaimed a moderate and reformist republican socialism, like the representatives of the Durkheimian school from Marcel Mauss to Maurice Halbwachs. Liberalism exerted a deep attraction on these 'state Jews'. Raymond Aron presented himself as a 'de-Judaized Jew', in other words, 'an unbeliever, nonpractising, of French culture, with no Jewish culture'.[22] The 'de-Judaized Jew', however, was not a heretic who had rejected any traditional heritage or been expelled from the synagogue, but a deeply assimilated Jew who had dissolved his faith into the civil religious of French republican nationalism. His political orientation was rather conformist; he was given to respect and idealize the prevailing institutions, despite his distance from conservatism, inasmuch as this was generally anti-republican and anti-Semitic. The French Israelites did not have the same conflictual relationship with the established authorities as the Jews of central Europe, excluded from higher education, senior administrative positions and the government parties. They did not even have the same relationship with the Jewish tradition, which they could profess in a secular form, with neither ruptures nor heresies. In 1940, Aron's republican patriotism led him to London, where he worked closely with General de Gaulle. After the war, however, his liberalism led him to denounce the 'opium of the intellectuals', and in 1968 to defend order against the '*chienlit*'.[23]

The 'state Jews' were an equally important phenomenon in Italy, where after the realization of national unity the small Israelite community experienced a dizzying socio-economic and political rise. In the model proposed by Antonio Gramsci and Arnaldo Momigliano, Jewish emancipation here was a particular aspect of the process of integrating various regional minorities into a single national entity. During the Risorgimento, Jews became Italians in the same sense as Sicilians, Piedmontese or Lombards.[24] Their linguistic and cultural assimilation coincided with that of these other Italians, and their integration into the nation's economic, political and intellectual elite happened in an almost natural way. As distinct from several other European countries, where emancipation followed the formation of states, in Italy Jews actively participated in the Risorgimento and contributed to building the national state. In 1874, four years after the fall of the Rome ghetto, the Italian parliament counted 15 Israelite deputies, a larger number than any other European parliament. In 1902, while France was still torn apart by the Dreyfus affair, the Italian government appointed a Jew to head the ministry of war, General Ottolenghi; then in 1915, Italy's entry into the war was prepared by an Israelite foreign minister, Sidney Sonnino. This simultaneity of socio-economic ascent, cultural assimilation and state integration favoured a certain intellectual and political conformism. Out of 26 Jewish deputies elected to parliament between the creation of the united Italian state and 1890, 20 belonged to the 'historic right'. Arnaldo Momigliano mentions in this respect the memory of his grandmother, an elderly Piedmontese lady who was carried away with emotion and burst into tears every time that she heard the royal march.[25] It was only natural that the Jewish elite should become fascist after 1922. In short, as distinct from the German model (social rise and institutional exclusion) or the French one (integration into a pre-existing state), the Italian model made Jews active subjects in the process of state construction.[26]

Anti-Semitism in Italy was driven above all by the church, the institution against which the Risorgimento had realized national unity; the church had made the monarchy its enemy. Instead of being viewed as a distinct community on account of its social and cultural practices, Jews were identified with a political elite and a state that a still embryonic nation (more than half the population did not speak standard Italian in the early twentieth century), economically backward and deeply influenced by the church, often perceived as an external authority. In 1938, the fascist regime's anti-Semitic turn (preceded by the reconciliation with the church in the Lateran pact and Mussolini's rapprochement with Nazi Germany) was experienced by the Jews as a trauma and a betrayal (exactly the same as with the change in the status of Jews in Vichy France). Political conformism, however, led the Italian Israelite community to reassert its loyalty to the 'fascist fatherland' and accept the 'painful sacrifices' it demanded. The major intellectual figure produced by Italian Judaism between the Risorgimento and fascism was perhaps Cesare Lombroso, founder of criminal anthropology and the perfect embodiment of positivist scientism and political conformism. Obsessed by craniology, he believed he had found the key to explain not only the hierarchy of races but also delinquency and anarchism. Jews were almost the only minority group for whom he claimed 'normal' status, escaping his scientistic clichés.[27]

In France, the tradition of 'state Jews' has continued through to today, with the one interruption under the Vichy regime, traumatic but short-lived. In central Europe, it never existed. In Germany, the liberal Jewish bourgeoisie produced bankers, industrialists, patrons of the arts, scholars, writers and journalists, but not statesmen. Zionism partly arose from this impossibility. If Theodor Herzl thought that a Jewish state would be the way to realize his dreams of grandeur, enabling him one day to address other sovereigns of the planet on an equal basis, this was partly because he was deeply aware of his exclusion from the Austrian aristocratic establishment. This rejection generated both forms of Jewish self-hatred[28] and an extreme form of Germanophilia. The historian Ernst Kantorowicz was fascinated by the aesthetic nationalism of the Stefan George circle, and took part in the repression of the Munich socialist republic in spring 1919,[29] in the ranks of the Freikorps. He was forced into exile in 1938, as was Hans-Joachim Schoeps, a Jewish pan-Germanist who greeted Hitler's arrival in power in 1933, hoping to convince him of the nationalism of his co-religionists.[30] This pathetic figure was not isolated. The chemist Fritz Haber, for example, was among the scientists who signed the famous appeal in support of German militarism in October 1914 (Haber also perfected the poison gases used at Ypres in 1915, and his name was placed on a list of war criminals at the end of the war).[31] Deeply tragic, on the other hand, was the fate of Walther Rathenau, dandy and aesthete, a brilliant intellectual and heir to the industrial giant AEG, a Prussian nationalist resigned to remain excluded from the military elite by reason of his

Jewishness, which, as he wrote in 1917, condemned him to live as a 'second-class citizen'.³² The Weimar republic finally seemed to grant him the recognition he had always sought, when he was appointed foreign minister in February 1922 as a member of the Democrat Party. Four months later, soon after the signing of the Rapallo treaty which normalized German-Soviet relations, he was assassinated in Berlin by a fanatical and anti-Semitic nationalist. During the weeks preceding his murder, the ranks of the Freikorps echoed with the slogan: '*Knall ab den Walther Rathenau, die gottverdammte Judensau!*' (Shoot down Walther Rathenau, the goddam Jewish sow).³³ Rathenau's tragic fate shows the insurmountable limits to any attempt at recognition based on a conservative and nationalist political option.

There was no place for a figure like Disraeli in interwar Germany. The affinities between the unfortunate Weimar foreign minister and Queen Victoria's prime minister were not negligible. Each of them admired the aristocracy, its style, values, tradition and institutions; each of them was a conservative, a fierce nationalist and a convinced orientalist, committed to his respective state's imperial policy; each idealized the racial principle; each was obsessed by an insatiable desire for recognition and honour; and each (the Englishman from the start, the Prussian towards the end of his life) proudly proclaimed his origins. Disraeli, the ennobled Tory politician, writer and essayist, was a kind of synthesis between Herzl and Rathenau.³⁴ But the anti-Semitism of Victorian England went no further than caricatures in the press, whereas the German equivalent did not shy away from murder. Rathenau's dream – to become a recognized and powerful statesman, the strategist of an imperial policy – would be realized after the Second World War by another German Jew, Henry Kissinger, but in the United States rather than in Germany.³⁵

As we have seen, the rise of state Jews in France and Italy was accompanied by the formation of a wide stratum of Israelite scholars, university professors, École Normale graduates, members of the Collège de France, *cattedrattici*. Paradoxically, the Jewish scientist who embodied the state ideal of the *Haskalah* did not triumph in Germany, the country that was the birthplace of this conception, but in France under the Third Republic. A gap thus opened between the two countries. In Germany, the scientist and the intellectual became two opposing figures, socially and politically distinct. There was a radical cleavage between the *Gelehrte* integrated into the Prussian empire, guardian of its values and doctrinal propagandist of its political conservatism, and the *Intellektuelle*, essayist and critic acting in a public sphere that emerged from the growing mass society, excluded from the university.[36] The former made the academy his fortress, whereas the latter wrote particularly for the press; the former embodied Germanness, the second was often Jewish. A favourite activity of the nationalists was to stigmatize different kinds of *littérateur* – *Zivilisationsliteraten*, *Kaffeehausliteraten*, etc. – whose common feature was clearly their Jewishness. In France, on the other hand, denunciation of the Jewish scientist was a commonplace of anti-Semitic propaganda: 'A Jew makes a horrible *polytechnicien* or *normalien*', wrote Drieu La Rochelle.[37] As distinct from Germany, where the figure of the scholar found its apotheosis in Max Weber, for whom the intellectual was basically just an irresponsible demagogue, in France it was represented by Émile Durkheim, the theorist of sociology as a positivist science, who had no hesitation in taking a stand in support of Captain Dreyfus in a controversy in which the Sorbonne clearly stood on the republican side.[38] The French intellectual was not necessarily an outsider, in a cultural space that did not have the German opposition between *Kultur* and *Zivilisation*.

In France, Jews were concentrated more in the world of science than that of the intellectual. After the Second World War, they would even be merciless lambasters of the 'opium of the intellectuals'. In this context, the figure of the intellectual, 'man of letters' and producer of ideas who intervened in public life to denounce injustices and abuses of power, the violence and oppression of the state, was symbolized by Jean-Paul Sartre. It was when the republic collapsed or was threatened by an authoritarian turn that the Jewish scientist turned intellectual: at the start of the century, the Durkheimian school became Dreyfusard; in 1940, Raymond Aron led France Libre in London; during the Algerian war, Pierre Vidal-Naquet denounced the torture and massacres of the French army. Far from being outsiders, these scientists were all patriots, like Marc Bloch, who in 1915 was prepared to die 'happily' for his country, or Raymond Aron who, in 1941, paid homage to Bergson by saluting him as the symbol of a patriotism 'tinged with mysticism', or again Pierre Vidal-Naquet, who proudly quoted the following passage from his father's diary: 'I receive as a Frenchman the insult made to me as a Jew.'³⁹ The identity of these Jewish scientists was summed up by Raymond Aron as follows: 'I am what is called an "assimilated Jew". As a child, I wept for the defeats of France at Waterloo and Sedan, not on hearing the tale of the destruction of the Temple. No other flag but the tricolour would ever moisten my eyes, and no other hymn but the Marseillaise.'⁴⁰ His Judaism had been 'revealed' by Hitler and he assumed it with dignity, but without taking any particular pride in it. These words, touching and sincere, are a thousand miles from the cosmopolitanism and 'pariah' internationalism of Rosa Luxemburg, Leo Trotsky or Isaac Deutscher, or from the conflict between Jewishness and Germanness that finds such acute expression in the writings of Gershom Scholem.

A variant of the Israelite French scientist today is what Elisabeth Roudinesco defines as the 'territory Jew'.⁴¹ This is the case with the historian Pierre Nora, who conceived and realized a vast 'heritage' project of the French past in his *Places of Memory*: an inventory drawn up in the era of globalization, when the profile of the nation was fading and the continuity of its story seemed threatened. The point, according to Nora, was to preserve a past that, cut off from the everyday lived experience of French people, and thus deprived of its natural vectors of transmission, took refuge in collective memory. This 'general topography of national memory' is akin to a sumptuous celebration, scholarly and nostalgic at the same time, of identity and rootedness. An undertaking in which some people have rightly perceived an 'erudition of patriotic appeasement'.⁴²

From empire to imperialism

A further source of Jewish liberalism lies in the cataclysms that so deeply struck central Europe between the two wars: the collapse of the multinational empires in 1918, the Shoah, then the massive transfers of population decided by the victor powers in 1945. When the Iron Curtain divided the continent, the exiles and survivors of the Holocaust were forced to choose their camp. Jewish cosmopolitanism then underwent a metamorphosis that led many orphans of *Mitteleuropa* to seek a substitute for this in Atlantic imperialism.⁴³ Several Jewish intellectuals from central Europe were among the leading lights in the Congress for Cultural Freedom, including Franz Borkenau and Arthur

Koestler, Richard Löwenthal, Manès Sperber and Friedrich Torbert. They had often started out as communists, and their Atlanticism was all the more zealous in that it bore the mark of apostasy.[44]

The great historian Salo W. Baron was the forerunner of this tendency. Born in 1895, in the Habsburg province of Galicia, he studied in Vienna and lost his nationality with the collapse of the Austrian empire. His *Social and Religious History of the Jews*, the magnum opus that he published in 1937, some ten years after his arrival in the United States, presented as a kind of 'historical law' the affinity of the Jews with great empires and multinational states, in which their 'foreignness' appeared 'less questionable'. In these states, 'the ubiquity of the Jews' could even constitute a cement helping to unite different groups around the state, as shown by historical examples from Islamic Spain to Carolingian Europe, the Polish monarchy and the Ottoman empire.[45] In 1814, Baron observed, the Congress of Vienna laid down a European order that proved far more reassuring and protective for Jews than did the nation-states established at Versailles in 1919.[46] Like many other émigrés, Baron saw the United States as a kind of imperial republic that was at the same time a multinational state able to offer protection to its various components, and particularly its Jewish minority. And it was a Jewish philosopher of German origin, son of an Orthodox rabbi from Prussian Silesia, Horace M. Kallen, who offered the first formulation of the concept of cultural pluralism. Kallen foresaw that the United States, after the upheaval of a century of waves of immigration, would inevitably be forced to abandon the conservative myth of a 'Wasp' nation and would come to see itself as 'a federal state not merely as a union of geographical and administrative unities, but also as a cooperation of cultural diversities, as a federation or commonwealth of national cultures'.[47]

The trajectory of Karl Popper, a Viennese Jew who emigrated to New Zealand in 1937, then to London in 1946, is another emblematic illustration of this tendency. The key element of continuity that linked the young Viennese socialist of the 1920s to the Cold War liberal of the 1940s, accompanying his transition from the philosophy of science to political philosophy, lay in his rejection of nationalism. Once central Europe had disappeared, his Habsburg cosmopolitanism gave way to an idealization of the British empire, seen as the cradle of Western liberalism. *The Open Society and Its Enemies* (1941) codified a view of the world in which the genealogy of modern totalitarianism found in Hegel the theorist of a 'neo-tribalism' whose ultimate culmination would be the Nazi *völkische Gemeinschaft*.[48] After the model of Athens, a democratic imperialism opposed to the authoritarianism of Sparta, the British empire had set itself up as the champion of liberty against totalitarian communism. The British 'Commonwealth' had revived the Habsburg cosmopolitanism, an 'open society' in which different nations, cultures and religions could coexist. According to Popper, from Alexander the Great to Churchill, by way of Napoleon, empires have been the vectors of progress in history. Popper rejected the principle of the nation-state, as 'none of the theories which maintain that a nation is united by a common origin, or a common language, or common history, is acceptable, or applicable in practice'. As a result, he concluded, the idea of the nation-state is 'an irrational myth'.[49] On this basis, and with a coherence that was lacking in other Jewish Cold War liberals, Popper radically opposed Zionism, seeing it as simply a regressive and anachronistic nationalism.[50]

The Zionism of Sir Isaiah Berlin, on the other hand, was unshakeable. Berlin, another key representative of the 'white emigration' that put its mark on postwar British culture, and ennobled eight years before Popper, also came from a multinational empire shattered by the Great War. Born in Riga in 1909, he belonged to a Jewish bourgeois family who had emigrated to England after the 1917 revolution. Berlin brought from his native land a deep love of Russian literature and a strong romantic sensibility. His liberalism identified with a British monarchy that had opened its doors to Jews – granting them a recognition they had never obtained in tsarist Russia – and gave an imperial tinge to his Baltic cosmopolitanism. Fascinated by Vico and Herder, of whom he was an admirable interpreter, he sought arguments for a redefinition of pluralism in their critique of natural right, universalism and rationalism: 'For Voltaire, Diderot, Helvétius, Holbach, Condorcet there is only universal civilization, of which now one nation, now another, represents the richest flowering. For Herder there is a plurality of incommensurable cultures.'[51] As his disciple John Gray has written, Berlin's project can be summed up as the quest for a synthesis between romanticism and liberalism, 'so reconciling the Enlightenment with its critics'.[52] The result was a conservative liberalism that opposed 'negative liberty' to 'positive liberty', individual freedom to democratic egalitarianism, by drawing on the tradition of the counter-Enlightenment.[53] Once embarked on this path, Berlin came upon the eighteenth-century German philosopher Johann Georg Hamann, of whom he drew an admiring portrait. Hamann was the first to launch a radical offensive against the Enlightenment, to reject the idea of a world without God, built on reason, populated by calculating minds, subject to explainable rational laws and freed forever from the enigmas of nature and faith. Against the disenchantment of a quantified world, Hamann rehabilitated the medieval idea of a man 'drunk on God', for whom everything is revelation. The Bible was all that he needed; ideas of determinism and causality, the certainties of science, were an irritation. He was categorically opposed to Voltaire, whose corrupting ideas aroused enthusiasm at the Prussian court. He admired Friedrich the Great but did not approve of his enlightened despotism, so marked by the harmful influence of 'political arithmeticians' from France. He also criticized Kant and Moses Mendelssohn, rejecting their idea of a *Rechtsstaat*. If people obeyed authority, thought Hamann (similarly to Bossuet and Joseph de Maistre), it is because this followed from a natural and divine order rather than from a logical one. His mixture of obscuranticism, populism, mysticism, irrationalism and anti-intellectualism watered the ground on which the flourishing plant of German nationalism, *völkisch* mythology and reactionary romanticism would arise a century later. From Fichte to Wagner, Treitschke to Spengler, every variant of cultural pessimism could rightly recognize Hamann as its spiritual father.

Isaiah Berlin was fascinated by Hamann; despite rejecting the latter's reactionary extremes, Berlin was not indifferent to the charm of his thought. On the one hand, he saw Hamann as the founder of modern irrationalism, 'the first standard-bearer and perhaps the most original figure' of a 'counter-revolution, which has cast alternate light and darkness upon the European scene'; on the other hand, he viewed him as firing 'the first great shot in the battle of the romantic individualists against rationalism and totalitarianism'.[54] According to Berlin, Hamann was both a precursor of fascism and its critic *avant la lettre*. In particular, he warned against the dogmatic rationalism of Voltaire and the like, for whom the world was composed of eternal and timeless truths, always identical to themselves and recognizable by the goddess Reason. In the wake of Jacob Talmon, another Jewish representative of liberal anti-communism and scourge of 'totalitarian democracy',[55] Berlin thought that the horrors of modernity flowed not just from fascist irrationalism but also from the emancipatory utopia of the Enlightenment, of which Rousseau was the spiritual father. For him, the author of the *Social Contract* was 'one of the most sinister and most formidable enemies of liberty in the whole history of modern thought';[56] Rousseau could equally be claimed by socialism, communism, authoritarianism, democratic liberalism and anarchism – anything except liberal civilization.

Isaiah Berlin's entire intellectual approach consisted in refounding liberalism in a conservative perspective, radically disassociating it from the emancipatory tradition of the Enlightenment which he rejected as a matrix of totalitarianism. Zeev Sternhell is not mistaken in the bold parallel with which he describes Berlin as the main representative of the anti-Enlightenment in the age of the Cold War: in the face of communism, he writes, 'Berlin assigned himself the role of Herder and Burke against the French Enlightenment.'[57] Berlin's pluralism led him to defend Zionism as the expression of a Jewish national particularity, but not to accept the presence in a British university of Marxist professors of Russian history. In 1963, he rejected the candidacy of Isaac Deutscher for a chair in Soviet studies at Sussex University, in words that admirably illustrate the contempt of the British-Jewish patriarchy for the 'non-Jewish Jews' of central Europe: the very idea of sharing 'the same academic community' with the biographer of Trotsky was for him 'morally intolerable'.[58] Far more respectable in his eyes was the Iranian dictator Reza Pahlavi, who in 1971 invited Berlin to celebrate the anniversary of Cyrus the Great in the ruins of Persepolis, the old imperial capital, where Berlin gave a lecture on the concept of liberty.[59] This would later be the theme of his Downing Street conversations with Margaret Thatcher.[60]

Neoconservatism

Among the consequences of the decline of anti-Semitism was the reconciliation between Jews and the political right. Begun in 1967, at the time of the Six Day War, this phenomenon was strengthened over the following decades, leading to what the Israeli philosopher Ivan Segré terms the 'philo-Semitic reaction'. The 'struggle against anti-Semitism' was integrated 'into the value system of an ideological current that was historically hostile to Jews'.[61] In this context, Jewish intellectuals ceased to embody, by virtue of their social position, an anti-conformist and critical minority; they became 'respectable' and were no longer perceived either as representatives of a negative alterity or as centres of subversion. They even sometimes became ideologists of the prevailing order.

This shift is well illustrated by the debate in recent years over the legacy of Leo Strauss. This conservative philosopher viewed modern political thought, from Machiavelli to the Enlightenment, as an inexorable decline into nihilism, of which Nazism was the extreme culmination. Conceiving political philosophy as a defence of universal and timeless truths, Strauss opposed the historicism, positivism and relativism of modern thought that found their expression in democracy – a weak and dangerous regime, as he believed was proved by the catastrophic experience of the Weimar republic that he had witnessed for himself during his youth in Germany.[62] His critique of modernity in the name of an ancient liberalism based on the valorization of moral virtues rather than on an idea of natural equality was also accompanied by a critique of Jewish secularization, of which Spinoza was the precursor, in the name of orthodoxy (and particularly of Maimonides).[63]

As distinct from Strauss, his disciples adopted more realistic positions, seeking to incorporate the master's values into a neoconservative political project. Athens and Jerusalem – reason and revelation, science and faith, philosophy and the Bible, the polis and the cradle of monotheisms – were for the Chicago thinker irreconcilable yet irreplaceable metaphors. Their tension was for him 'the secret of the vitality of Western civilization' – its theological and political kernel – condemned to seek an impossible synthesis.[64] Strauss's disciples believed they had overcome this contradiction by the alliance between America and Israel, the homeland of liberty and the homeland of the Jews. Athenian democracy had shifted to Washington, and ancient Judaism had taken a secular form in the state of Israel.[65] On this path, the Straussians initially encountered the descendants of another intellectual current, in this case springing from Marxism, and transmigrated with these people (Irving Kristol, Norman Podhoretz, James Burnham) to a radical anti-communism during the years of McCarthyism, finally uniting with the fundamentalist (and philo-Zionist) Christian right in a new and paradoxical alliance. In short, the neoconservative Jewish intelligentsia transformed universalism into Occidentalism.

In this vision, the West signified liberty, a value that had to be defended against the assault of the new barbarians. The Straussians thus linked up with an older neoconservative tradition which projected the ideas of Carl Schmitt – politics as domain of confrontation between friend and enemy – in the context of the Cold War, then that of the war against Islam. The first to champion this orientation, in the 1940s, was another German-Jewish intellectual who had emigrated to America, Hans Morgenthau, theorist of political realism, who had been a disciple of Carl Schmitt in Berlin, before ten years later joining the US State Department under George F. Kennan.[66] More recently, the same view has been reformulated by the neoconservative political scientist Samuel Huntington in terms of the 'clash of civilizations'.[67] This set of ideas and orientations inspired the foreign policy of George W. Bush in his two presidential terms, its strategists being called by the media the 'Straussian connection'. Among these declared Straussians were the deputy defense secretary Paul Wolfowitz, the Pentagon official Abram Shulsky, the Middle East presidential adviser Elliot Abrams and the strategist of the war on Iraq, Richard Perle.[68] Without being a direct member of this cohort, the international relations specialist Robert Kagan, one of the conceivers of the 'project for a new American century', theorized the imperial mission of the United States by supplying the arguments that served to justify the war on Iraq. Rediscovering the Hobbesian concept of sovereignty – the Leviathan as pact of union and submission – he conferred on the United States the role of laying down a new international order and guaranteeing the protection and security of nations in exchange for their submission to American power.[69]

Jewish neoconservatism did not just find expression among political strategists. Its presence is also visible in other disciplines, and in the cultural debate that followed the publication of *The Closing of the American Mind* (1988), the bestseller of another disciple of Strauss, Allan Bloom, who simultaneously denounced the nihilism of the human sciences, in an academy dominated by deconstruction and postmodern relativism, and the decadence of manners, of which rock music was the symptom, in a context of global social crisis comparable to the agony of the Weimar republic.[70]

Ruptures

This metamorphosis did not happen at a single stroke. During the 1960s and 1970s, Jews were still broadly aligned with the left. The tradition of critical thought created over a century and a half remained solid both in Europe and the United States. In France, the identification of the Jewish youth with leftism became a media cliché, with the joke that the reason that prevented the leaders of the Ligue Communiste Révolutionnaire from holding their meetings in Yiddish was that one of them, Daniel Bensaïd, was of Sephardic origin. Several intellectuals who reached maturity and developed their work in the postwar years, from Pierre Vidal-Naquet to Jacques Derrida, had personal experience of anti-Semitism and persecution during the war. Other younger ones followed and tried to renew this tradition, but its soil had already dried up.

The first rupture between Jews and the left took place in McCarthyite America, when a stratum of intellectuals who had been radicalized in the 1930s under the impact of the capitalist crisis lost hope and transformed their anti-Stalinism into anti-communism. This was the trajectory of a number of New York intellectuals who had been subject to Trotsky's influence, a large proportion of these being Jewish; some went on to become leading figures of neoconservatism (Sidney Hook, Irving Kristol, Felix Morrox, Nathan Glazer, Lionel Trilling, Ellot Cohen and Saul Bellow). One of their main mouthpieces was the journal *Commentary*, founded in 1945 by the American Jewish Committee.[71] In Europe, the rift occurred later, in 1967, at the time of the Six Day War. This event, in the words of the Italian poet Franco Fortini, destroyed the idea that 'Judaism, anti-fascism, Resistance and socialism were close to one another'. Judaism, he continued, being 'indissociable from an immense persecution and not yet explored in all its dimensions', seemed to 'sum up all persecution in itself'.[72] The second Arab-Israeli war – the first, in 1948, had seemed a struggle of survival for Israel, and was supported by the USSR and the left – destroyed this illusion.

The shift became particularly visible in the 1980s. Some analysts have stressed the presence of a large number of Jewish intellectuals among the 'new reactionaries'.[73] Others have rejoiced in this metamorphosis, such as the American neoconservative Martin Kramer, for whom the Jews, after ceasing to strengthen the ranks of revolutionary movements, have finally become a 'status quo people'.[74] As German-speaking central Europe was the cradle of Jewish critical thought between emancipation and the Holocaust, so France and the United States are today the centres of a new conservative Jewish intelligentsia. For two or three generations of Jewish intellectuals, communism was the secular version of an old messianic hope. After the Second World War, with the first wave of anti-communism in the 1950s, this aspiration shifted to the defence of the 'free world', then, from the 1990s, to the unconditional defence of Israel.

At the price of a somewhat risky sociological short cut, it is tempting to interpret this phenomenon in the light of the dialectic between 'established' and 'marginal' described by Norbert Elias,[75] though such an explanation must remain approximate. In the majority of cases, Jewish neoconservatives are neither scientists in the classic sense nor intellectuals, though they sometimes like to echo this posture in a caricature version (instead of Zola's *J'accuse*, Bernard-Henri Lévy's 'Tobruk oath'). Their 'authority' and influence are based neither on their status as producers of knowledge nor on the importance of their literary or scientific work, but essentially on the strategic position they occupy in the culture industry, in an age of commodity reification of the public sphere.[76] Masters of the communication codes, they are perfectly adapted to the constraints of the videosphere, and know how to combine writing with speech and image, making their works consumer products for promotion simultaneously in the press, on radio and on television.

The rejection of anti-Semitism and the political integration of Jews into the Western world did not lead to a dissolution of their alterity but, paradoxically, to its valorization. The old stigma was transformed into a mark of distinction, giving way, says Peter Novick, to a 'particularist ethos' perfectly compatible with the social and political order.[77] Elie Wiesel's famous expression, defining the Holocaust as 'a unique tragedy with universal implications', translates very well this coexistence between an ethnocentrism of a new type and a Western universalism.[78] We thus have a rhetoric around the 'Jewish signifier', the name of Jew and its 'transcendence', its universality and its 'original election', which would have horrified Jewish revolutionaries before the Holocaust, and in which Hannah Arendt saw, already in 1942, a secular form of Judeocentrism, if not a 'variant of racist superstition'.[79] The Israeli critic Yitzhak Laor expressed his irritation at this invasive philo-Semitism that seems to have conquered a Europe that makes demands of 'the Jew and his past' and is finally prepared to recognize him as its legitimate representative.[80]

The end of a cycle

After Auschwitz, anti-Semitism ceased to be the dominant modality of the perception of Jewish alterity in European societies. A sense of guilt gradually replaced the ancient contempt. Jews abandoned their old condition of pariah and acquired a fully legitimate position in the continent's cultural and political institutions. Already apparent in the nineteenth century, at least in Victorian England, this tendency blossomed after the Second World War without meeting any new obstacles. In other words, Jews remained, in Slezkine's definition, representatives of modernity, but they ceased to constitute a target and scapegoat. In the globalized world, diasporic minorities do not always swim against the current. Jews thus ceased to be 'foreigners' in the age of the 'universal triumph of Mercury'.[81] In a certain sense, the Shoah closed a cycle of European intellectual history, in which Jews had been at the heart. Between the late nineteenth century and the 1930s, Berlin, Vienna and Paris were centres of an intellectual flourishing quite comparable, in its brilliance and influence, with that of Athens in the fifth and fourth centuries BC, Muslim Andalusia before the reconquest, Renaissance Italy or seventeenth-century Amsterdam. The Holocaust put an end to an age in which, to use the words of Eric Hobsbawm, Jews underwent an explosion of creativity, like boiling water lifting the lid of a saucepan.[82] But the end of pariah Judaism also meant the end of the stage in the history of critical thought in the Western world.

The historical conditions that had placed Jews at the heart of this critical thought ceased to exist after 1945. On the one hand, the Holocaust destroyed (sometimes completely) the Jewish presence in several countries, such as Germany, Austria and Poland, where their intellectual role had been decisive before the war. On the other hand, the integration of the Shoah into European historical consciousness had a cathartic effect by banishing anti-Semitism from the state apparatus, the public sphere and cultural institutions. In parallel with this, the birth of the state of Israel, whose alliance with the great Western powers was consolidated over the decades, changed both the identity of the Jewish diaspora and its conditions of existence. The Jewish world polarized around two fundamental points of reference, the memory of the Shoah and support for Israel: the new 'civil religion' of human rights and the vanguard of the West in the Arab world. The former trouble-makers and disrupters of order had become its pillars.

The conservative revolution, alternately a critique of modernity, a complaint about decadence and an apology for force, continued to combine defence of tradition with the cult of authority, often with a fascination for technology. Neoconservatism always ends up in an apologia for the West. David Landes has reconstituted the history of capitalism as a brilliant illustration of the superiority of the West over other civilizations, swapping the Weberian diagnosis of the 'iron cage' for a smug apology for neoliberal globalization, and mocking all those who reproach this Eurocentrism: he 'prefers truth to fine feelings'.[83] The Islamologist Bernard Lewis asked 'what went wrong' in Islam to prevent it from assimilating the Western model, archetype of modernity.[84] Ruth Wisse, for her part, sets out to harmonize Zionism with the most extreme Occidentalism, attributing to Israel a key role in the crusade against Islam and all obscurantisms opposed to democracy. She also manages to find a synthesis between Zionism and the old vision of the royal alliance: Israel as guide and avant-garde of American imperialism, its protector.[85]

The concept of the West has always been vague. For the last two centuries it denoted several different and sometimes contradictory things. In the nineteenth century, imperialism identified itself with Europe's 'civilizing mission' to legitimize its colonial enterprise. From Oswald Spengler to Samuel Huntington, it indicates a view of a unique civilization opposed to its enemies. Its cultural and geographical boundaries are vague and fluctuating. Some liberals equate it with the market and democracy, despite the fact that in the course of the twentieth century, the latter has been several times overthrown – from republican Spain to Mossadegh's Iran and Allende's Chile – in the name of defending Western interests or even values. Fundamentalists see the West as a product of Christianity, obliterating a centuries-long history that made Europe a melting-pot of civilizations. For a melancholic conservative such as Tocqueville, the West was summed up by its vocation to dominate.[86] The birth of Jewish neoconservatism adds a new component to this, from a tradition that historically it had always perceived as hostile.

4
Between Two Epochs: Jewishness and Politics in Hannah Arendt

Hannah Arendt occupies a singular and unclassifiable place, both in political theory and contemporary Jewish culture. Belonging neither to the left nor the right, she escapes traditional categorizations. We could even say that she does not fall into any of the broad tendencies analysed up to now: neither a 'non-Jewish Jew', since she displayed an acute awareness of her Jewishness from her student years in the Weimar republic onwards, nor a representative of conservatism. Her work, however, reflects in its way the influence of both. Her most famous book, *The Origins of Totalitarianism* (1951), forms a dividing line between two stages in her intellectual and political trajectory: the first dominated by reflection on Jewish history in the light of the concept of 'pariah'; the second oriented towards the elaboration of a theory of the public sphere and freedom (far more abstract and disembodied). We can see this as a separation between the two moments of her experience, one European and the other American: the first concerned with struggle against oppression, the second to define the framework of an achieved freedom, sometimes at the price of indifference to new forms of domination and new emancipatory struggles. This transition illustrates the turn that Jewish modernity made, and thus justifies – beyond the importance of Arendt's own work – the choice of devoting a separate chapter to her.

In 1959, when the city of Hamburg awarded her the Lessing prize, Hannah Arendt delivered a lecture with a strong autobiographical accent, entitled: 'On Humanity in Dark Times'. Some ten years later, she collected under this title a series of essays on the intelligentsia in the twentieth century, to which the Hamburg lecture served as introduction.[1] This title perfectly grasps the deep kernel of Arendt's existential itinerary, aware as she was of belonging to a humanity cast into the maelstrom of wars and totalitarianisms, which had almost devoured it and from which it had not emerged unscathed. The 'dark times' of the twentieth century were in fact indissociable from her political thought. It was in this European crisis, whose impact on the Jewish world we have already seen, that the founding experience of her thought has to be sought. In a letter to Karl Jaspers of January 1946, she recognized this openly, writing: 'I have refused to abandon the Jewish question as the focal point of my historical and political thinking.'[2] This 'question' – a set of experiences and problems, including anti-Semitism, the crisis of the nation-state, persecution, exile, cosmopolitanism, with its tragic epilogue in the Shoah – thus constituted, in many respects, the matrix of her political theory.

Arendt came from the German philosophical tradition, as she herself indicated in a famous letter to Gershom Scholem that we shall return to later. Martin Heidegger and Karl Jaspers were her teachers, and her youth was filled with philosophical reading, from the Greek classics to Kant and Hegel. The attempts to tie Arendt's thought to Heideggerian ontology, whether as mere disciple or inflexible critic, reducing her work to a tormented confrontation, either apologetic or destructive, with the author of *Being and Time*, are not very fruitful.[3] Her intellectual relationship with Heidegger evolved over the years in a winding trajectory, not to say an incoherent one. Her rejection of political existentialism, which commenced at the time of her exile from Germany in 1933, became explicit in a 1946 essay in which Heidegger's famous *Dasein* is presented as a linguistic ruse enabling him to evacuate the concept of 'humanity', with the result that 'all the characteristics of man that Kant had provisionally sketched under the terms of liberty, human dignity and reason' disappeared.[4] In 1953, after a reconciliation with her former teacher, she qualified this contention, attributing Heidegger's adherence to Nazism to his naivety and his lack of character rather than to his thought. In a passage from her *Denktagebuch*, she defines him as a clumsy 'fox', always ready to 'prowl around the traps that others set for him' until the day that his damaged fur no longer provides any protection and he decides to construct his own trap in the form of a hole, in which he establishes himself after having 'disguised it as a regular foxhole'.[5] Finally, in 1969, on the occasion of Heidegger's eightieth birthday, she delivered an astonishing apology for the German philosopher, now presenting his adhesion to Nazism simply as an 'escapade'. Heidegger's 'error', attributed here to the 'attraction to the tyrannical' so typical of 'many great thinkers', was insufficient in her eyes to tarnish the reputation of a thought that, drawing its sources in the 'immemorial', rose like a 'storm' far stronger than those that agitated his century.[6] In studying Arendt's political thought, we have to recognize her debt towards her teacher, in the context of a complex and ambiguous relationship in which personal affection was combined with intellectual fascination and could interfere with political judgement. It would however be reductive to seek to imprison Arendt solely in this confrontation with the Messkirch philosopher. Her political philosophy is original and unclassifiable. German philosophy certainly forms the background of her work, but this transcends all filiation, going beyond legacies, breaking traditions, reformulating old lines of questioning and creating new concepts. On the intellectual level, Arendt was above all a product of the 'dark times' of her century, an age of extremes of which Germany was the epicentre. The stages of her intellectual and political formation are the same as those that marked the European collapse: Nazism, and the exile, persecution and genocide of the Jews.

Pariah Judaism

The great turning-point was 1933. For Arendt, the advent of Nazism marked her discovery of politics, or rather her transition from philosophy to politics. During the years that followed, pure philosophical speculation – for example that which inspired her essay on Augustine's concept of love (1929) – was no longer possible. It was only towards the end of her life, in America, that she rediscovered the serenity needed for this type of reflection. From the 1930s onwards, Arendt viewed the world through a political prism. This metamorphosis resulted from the trauma of 1933, but the paths that she took were completely her own. Hannah Arendt's formation was not within the German left; she did not experience the influence of Marxism that was so powerful at this time, as she emphasized in her letter to Scholem, adding that she did not see this as a reason for pride. In her discovery of politics – or rather the impossibility of thinking outside of politics – she did not move in this direction, though it was the one taken by Günther Anders and Heinrich Blücher, her two husbands. In other words, her itinerary did not coincide with that of a large number of intellectuals of her generation. Her particular choice, at the same time clearly anti-Nazi and irreducible to the political stands of her time, would not be devoid of consequences. Her discovery of politics did not flow from a reflection on the nature of fascism or the historical defeat of the German workers' movement, the most powerful and most organized in western Europe. It was born out of her reflection on the Jewish question, which was precisely one of the blind spots of Marxism.

In the wake of many German Jews of her generation, Arendt was born into a milieu that was completely secular, and she did not receive any religious education.[7] She did not learn Hebrew, did not attend the synagogue and was not familiar with the theological controversies of the early 1920s that interested the young Erich Fromm, tormented Siegfried Kracauer and Max Horkheimer and inspired Martin Buber and Franz Rosenzweig. As a daughter of the Enlightenment, Arendt never regretted having been born into a profoundly secular family. Judaism in its religious forms seemed to her a legacy from the past, more or less obsolete and basically of no interest. Her correspondence with Scholem – both her letters of 1947 on the foundation of the state of Israel and those of 1963 on the Eichmann trial – shows two remote and incompatible languages, often leading to misunderstanding or incomprehension. The key dividing line lies precisely in the religious interpretation of Judaism, to which the historian of the Jerusalem Kabbalah rallied but which the New York exile rejected. For Arendt, Nazi anti-Semitism was the point of departure for neither a theological anamnesis nor a discovery of Judaism in its national forms. Born in Königsberg, she was familiar with the thought of Kant and completely foreign to *Yiddishkeit*, a culture towards which she displayed the indifference or even prejudice that was typical of German Jews. But no more did Arendt rally to political Zionism, despite establishing a relationship of critical collaboration with this in the 1930s and 1940s. During this dramatic time, thinking the Jewish question meant acknowledging the end of the 'German-Jewish symbiosis', the aporias of assimilation, the shipwreck of emancipation and *Aufklärung*. It also meant bringing to light the 'hidden tradition' of pariah Judaism. In an early essay, written in 1932, Arendt already displays a great interest in the Jewish intelligentsia of the late eighteenth century, on the eve of emancipation. She was particularly fascinated by the figure of Rahel Levin Varnhagen, whose Berlin salon was the most famous of its day, and whose biography Arendt wrote during the years of her exile in

France.⁸ As an intellectual, woman and Jew, Arendt felt a strong affinity for Rahel. Both had lived at a time of transition, Rahel Varnhagen at the dawn of the long cycle of emancipation, and Hannah Arendt at its dusk. In 1933, the Jewish condition had once again become that of a 'pariah people', as it had been in the days of the Berlin hostess. Rahel's salon had been a model of sociability in the private sphere, outside the public institutions but at the same time at the centre of German intellectual life, a place where Jews could meet gentiles and discuss with them on a basis of equality, in the name of a common cultural adherence. Arendt's Berlin, on the other hand, was a world in which Jews had acquired a leading cultural position, but where, struck by an anti-Semitism that once again deprived them of their rights, they were excluded once more.

Max Weber, in his *Sociology of Religion*, coined the concept of a 'pariah people' (*Paria-Volk*) to define the 'negative privileges' of the Jews, in other words the various forms of discrimination they experienced in Christian Europe across the centuries. By analogy with a group denoted as 'impure' and therefore struck by ritual prohibitions, the German sociologist characterized Jews as a kind of 'caste' in a world without the caste system.⁹ But it was particularly thanks to the writings of Bernard Lazare, the defender of Captain Dreyfus and author of *Job's Dunghill* (1927), that Arendt explored the figure of the pariah Jew during her years in France. For Lazare, the pariah was not simply someone excluded; he was the proscribed who transforms himself into rebel, who does not accept passively suffering his oppressed condition but makes it the point of departure for a political revolt. In other words, a 'conscious pariah'.¹⁰ At the antipode to the pariah, and in a certain sense his dialectical double, was the figure of the parvenu, the Jew who seeks to escape his condition by getting round it, exorcising it, feigning not to notice it, not combatting his oppressors but identifying with them in several forms of mimetism. Bernard Lazare found traces of this pathetic figure in Theodor Herzl, the founder of political Zionism, who conceived a future Jewish nation in Palestine after the model of the Prussian empire, and dreamt of being admitted to the European aristocracy.¹¹ Arendt also saw its archetype in a certain conservative Jewish patriarchate, champion of an intensified German nationalism by which it sought to make up for its own defective lineage.

In tracing her portrait of the Jewish parvenu, Arendt did no more than describe the attitude of the German-Jewish elite, several representatives of which she knew personally. This elite reacted to the rise of Nazism in a contradictory way, taking up positions that, a posteriori, appear irrational or blind, but which reflect the surprise, disarray and impotence of a group struck by an unexpected catastrophe for which it was not prepared. Before being persecuted or driven into exile, Jewish notables were divided between sarcastic contempt for the new rulers of Germany and a complete prostration that was neither courageous nor effective. The first attitude was that of Freud who, summoned to declare publicly that he had not suffered any ill-treatment when he prepared to leave Vienna in 1938, wrote an ironic text in which he cordially recommended the Gestapo to all his fellow-citizens. The second was that of the representatives of the Zentralverein, the representative body of the Judaic community, which reasserted their unshakeable loyalty to the German state: an attitude that took a caricatured and grotesque accent among Jewish pan-Germanists such as Max Neumann, when they approved the nationalist turn proclaimed by Hitler.[12] Hannah Arendt was very familiar with this mental habitus, made up of conformism and submission to authority. Max Arendt, her grandfather, had been a member of the Zentralverein in Königsberg, and a regular visitor to his house was the young Kurt Blumenfeld, who maintained friendly relations with Arendt after his conversion to Zionism. In March 1933, Blumenfeld protested vigorously, in a telegram sent to the American Jewish Committee in New York, against any manifestation of hostility towards Germany.[13] A large number, particularly on the left, thought that the gains of emancipation were irreversible, and that all that was needed to quiet Hitler was to convince him that German Jews were authentic nationalists.

Against this posture, Arendt rediscovered the 'hidden tradition' of pariah Judaism, rich despite the memory hole into which political conformism had relegated it, that had always been another dimension of Jewish modernity. In an essay of 1944, she illustrated this in a gallery of portraits, from Heinrich Heine to Bernard Lazare, Charlie Chaplin and Franz Kafka.[14] The pages she devotes to the humanity of the pariah are among the finest in twentieth-century literature. Lacking a personal inheritance, the pariah attributes great importance to friendship. Excluded from the public sphere and deprived of rights, he finds a ray of light in the human warmth of his neighbours. Excluded from any form of citizenship, he rediscovers humanity as a universal category, transcending laws and political frontiers. Love, sensitivity, generosity, the sense of fraternity and solidarity, the absence of prejudice, Arendt emphasizes, are human qualities that in these dark times find a refuge among the pariahs, the proscribed and those without rights. As a consequence, pariahs have always been enemies of power, anti-conformists, rebels, creators, the embodiment of the critical spirit.[15]

Such a surplus of humanity, however, is simply a reaction to the lack of rights. In her essay on Kafka, Arendt quotes a passage from *The Castle* that metamorphoses the condition of the pariah Jew in the 1930s: 'You are not of the Castle and you are not of the village, you are nothing at all.'[16] In short, the other face of the pariah's humanism is the deprivation of rights, public invisibility, exclusion from political life. Persecution can bring the oppressed together, by producing 'a warmth of human relationships… [which is] an almost physical phenomenon'. It remains, however, that the condition of this pariah humanity is 'worldlessness', in other words, a 'fearful atrophy of all the organs with which we respond to [the world]'. The pariah, in other words, lives the condition of genuine 'worldlessless' (*Weltlosigkeit*), which is 'always a form of barbarism'.[17]

In the wake of a long literary tradition – the first references to the pariah in Western dictionaries go back to the early seventeenth century – the pariah has often been reduced to a moral category, an object of compassion, or an aesthetic figure, the artist and bohemian. For Arendt, however, this is an eminently political category that denotes those women and men excluded from citizenship, who lack 'the right to have rights'.[18] In the twentieth century, pariahs are stateless par excellence, individuals 'without a state', refugees and exiles. This definition follows in a tradition that goes back to the beginnings of the French Revolution, when the concept of pariah was already used as a rhetorical figure to refer to various categories excluded because of their sex (women), religion (Jews) or social function (domestic servants). In the nineteenth century, Flora Tristan conferred on it an aspect of rebellion. 'In the figure of the pariah,' writes Eleni Varikas, 'there is thus an encounter between the political and social dimensions of alterity that denotes (and denounces) the procedures of distancing the other… and the romantic dimension, no less political, of individual identity as representation of the subject in revolt.'[19] In other words, the pariah does not just express an objective condition of experienced exclusion, but also a subjectivity that proudly proclaims his condition and makes it into the source of a challenge to the established order and a banner against the injustices of the world. As Varikas goes on to say, this refers to a self-representation sometimes tinged with narcissism (which Bernard Lazare calls 'the pride of the pariah' and 'the pleasure of being hated').[20] Arendt, however, seems not to have known of this tradition, as the names of Zalkind Hourwitz, Mary Wollstonecraft, Anacharsis Cloots and Flora Tristan do not appear in her writing. Her link to it was through Bernard Lazare as intermediary, discovering through him a use of the concept that transcended the limits of Weberian sociology. She in turn used it in an essentially political sense. During the 1930s and 1940s, Jews were a kind of 'ideal type' of the pariah, but in Arendt's eyes this category was far wider, denoting a figure born of the European postwar crisis, when the collapse of the old multinational empires gave birth to a mosaic of fragile national states, heterogeneous and deeply unstable. The peace treaties made at the Versailles conference ratified the ethnic purges begun during the Great War, decided on forced transfers of populations and traced frontiers that were often artificial. Revolutions, counter-revolutions and finally the advent of fascism created a growing mass of refugees, stateless people for whom the League of Nations proved impotent. There were millions who had lost their legal status and national identity in the wake of the collapse of the old European order. These pariahs, Arendt explained, were treated like outlaws, not because they had transgressed but because the law did not recognize them, condemning them thus to political invisibility and 'worldlessness', as if they were 'superfluous' individuals.[21]

Zionism

To maintain that the 'Jewish question' forms the matrix of Hannah Arendt's political thought requires certain qualifications. As distinct from theologians or nationalists, Arendt saw Jewishness neither as the religion of a 'chosen people' nor as an ontological category, but rather as a historical condition that summed up the crisis of the old world and demanded a political solution. For her, it was a historically determined existential condition, not a filiation that compelled religious obligations or community constraints. Consequently, her relationship with Zionism was always very tense. First of all, dialogue and collaboration but marked by a certain autonomy of judgement, then rupture and the taking of an increasingly critical distance. The red thread that accompanied this shift was her attachment to the universal idea of humanity, which rejected any form of nationalism. Not familiar with the history of the Yiddish-speaking community, the bearer of a national culture and a rich socialist tradition – the Bund was founded in 1897 in the tsarist empire – Arendt viewed Zionism as a first attempt to transform Jews into political subjects able to claim their rights and combat anti-Semitism. That was why she lent it critical support, first of all by working in Paris for an association that organized the emigration of Jewish children to Palestine, then waging a campaign during the war, particularly with her articles in *Aufbau*, the German-language Jewish weekly published in New York, for the creation of a 'Jewish army' for the struggle against Nazism. In concrete terms, this meant forming Jewish units within the Allied military forces. Since Hitlerite Germany had designated Jews as its particular enemy, they would thereby have had the sense of participating directly as such in the war, without the mediation of the states that had given them refuge (but where they rarely had the status of citizens). This combat implied a radical shift in the mental habitus that Jews had formed for themselves over the centuries, and which, after emancipation, had championed assimilation and identification with the various European nations. 'The Jewish people,' Arendt wrote in November 1941,

> are beginning to learn... that *you can only defend yourself as the person you are attacked as*. A person attacked as a Jew cannot defend himself as an Englishman or Frenchman. The world would only conclude that he is simply not defending himself. Perhaps this precept of political battle has now been learned by those tens of thousands of French Jews who feared a 'Jewish war' and thought they had to defend themselves as Frenchmen, only to end up separated from their French fellow warriors and interned in Jewish prison camps in Germany.[22]

In May 1942, a year before the Warsaw ghetto uprising, she formulated the idea of a struggle for self-emancipation consisting in the attempt to 'replace the rules of extermination and the rules of flight with the rules of battle'.[23]

If the realization of this project made Zionism an indispensable interlocutor, Arendt did not thereby give up her principled hostility towards a Jewish state, in this time of historic crisis for nation-states. The strategy that the Zionist movement stubbornly pursued during the war, which consisted in presenting the colonization of Palestine as the only effective way to oppose Nazism, was viewed by Arendt, writing in December 1941, as 'a dangerous folly' (*ein gefährliche Wahn*).[24] In the first years after the war, she took part in debates in the association Brit Shalom (Alliance for Peace) – inspired by such eminent figures as the philosopher Martin Buber, the founder of the Jerusalem university Yehuda Leib Magnes, the sociologist Arthur Ruppin and Gershom Scholem – which championed the idea of a binational Jewish-Arab state in Palestine.[25] The foundation of Israel, however, finally accepted by the majority of members of this association, encountered her principled hostility. This was the cause of a first break with Scholem, who accused her, in a letter of 1946, of adopting a Trotskyist kind of internationalism.[26] The polemical force of Arendt's writings at this time is reminiscent in many ways of the devastating critique that Bernard Lazare had made of Theodor Herzl 40 years earlier.[27]

Re-reading today an article like 'Zionism Reconsidered', written in November 1944 in the wake of an American Zionist convention in Atlantic City that had adopted the programme of a Jewish state over the whole of the Palestinian territory, we are struck by its premonitory character.[28] A Jewish state, Arendt wrote at this time, could only be established in Palestine on two conditions, both problematic: on the one hand, by expelling the Palestinians from their lands; on the other, by transforming the Arab population within its borders into a mass of second-class citizens, culturally foreign and integrated into a political community towards which they would never be able to feel a sense of belonging. A few years later, in a passage of her famous work on totalitarianism, Arendt indicated that the foundation of Israel had been the act of birth of a new category of Palestinian pariahs.[29] Once again, the status of pariah was not bound up with the 'essence' of a people, but was a particular and changing historical condition.

Basically, according to Arendt, Zionism was strangely symmetrical to the radical assimilation championed by Judaism after emancipation; for the German, French and Italian Jewish elites, Jews had ceased to be a nation and become completely identified with their respective countries; while, for the Zionists, the Jews were a nation that needed its own state in order to exist. According to Arendt, they all remained imprisoned by the paradigm of the nation-state in an age when this had proved its historical bankruptcy by two world wars.

To Scholem, who proclaimed his nationalism and finally came round to accepting the foundation of Israel despite his 'anarchist' attitude to the state, Arendt recalled that 'the nation, or rather the nation-state as organization of peoples' was irremediably 'dead', and that, as a consequence, 'a Jewish national state would be a stupid and dangerous joke' (*ein gefährlicher und dummer Spass*).[30] The alternative, for her, lay in a dissociation between the state form and the principle of nationality. From this point of view, a binational Jewish-Arab state should form part of a federation of Middle Eastern peoples. Since this was never a concrete political option, Arendt's federalism always remained very vague, never taking a clear institutional form. During the Second World War, however, she seemed to view the Soviet federal system with great interest, and even a certain sympathy. True, the USSR was a totalitarian regime, but 'one thing has to be admitted: the Russian Revolution found an entirely new and – as far as we can see today – an entirely just way to deal with nationality or minorities. This new historic fact is that for the first time in modern history, an identification of nation and state has not even been attempted.'[31] Written in 1943, at a time when Stalinism had restored Great Russian nationalism and was preparing to deport whole peoples suspected of collaboration with the Nazi occupation, this passage displays a naive optimism, of which scarcely any trace remains in her later work. It does however attest to an interest for the socialist idea of a supranational community capable of breaking the logic of the nation-state (or of protected minorities). Very likely, the main source of information that Arendt had on the subject of Soviet federalism was her husband, the dissident German communist Heinrich Blücher. In any case, her approach is also reminiscent of the theory of national-cultural autonomy elaborated by Otto Bauer, Simon Dubnov and the Bund,[32] though she was probably never aware of these earlier debates.

The Holocaust

Exile for Hannah Arendt was a fundamental experience, bound up with her status as a persecuted Jew, a theme echoed in many of her writings. A 1943 article, 'We Refugees', strikes a similar tone to *Minima Moralia*, the collection of fragments written at the same time in which Theodor W. Adorno calls exile a 'damaged life'.[33] Arendt and Adorno both described exile as a world of both material and spiritual deprivation, made up of poverty, precariousness, abandonment of a stable profession and the impossibility of inhabiting one's own language. For Adorno, exile was above all the loss of a *Heimat* conceived as a spiritual shelter. Arendt found the kernel of exile in the political impotence bound up with the condition of being stateless. The 'wordlessness' of the exile, however, was compensated for on the intellectual level by an epistemological privilege of which both Adorno's and Arendt's writings of the 1940s are the most solid evidence. Torn away from the social and political fabric of his world of origin, suspended in a void of extra-territoriality and 'fluctuating freely',[34] the exiled intellectual escaped the dominant mental habitus, national stereotypes and conventions.

It was precisely this pariah sensibility that made Hannah Arendt, during the war and amid a world that was blind and indifferent, a remarkably lucid analyst of Jewish extermination. In 1946, she described the Nazi 'death factories' in which human beings reduced to a 'monstrous equality without fraternity or humanity' were 'killed like cattle', reflecting 'the image of hell'.[35]

Arendt viewed the world with the eyes of the Jewish exile torn away from a continent that had been transformed into a deadly trap. She did not look at the world with the eyes of the Americans, for whom the main enemy was Japan, nor those of the Europeans, who witnessed without reacting this tragic epilogue to the long history of anti-Semitism. But neither did she view it from the perspective of the Jewish institutions. For Orthodox Judaism, Nazism was simply the nth persecution, proof of an age-old Jewish vocation for suffering and martyrdom. For Zionism, particularly myopic in this tragic context, the struggle against anti-Semitism in Europe distracted precious energy from the struggle for Jewish colonization in Palestine, a struggle in which the main obstacle was presented by the British mandate authority set on limiting Jewish immigration. The exiles, on the other hand, perceived the war as the end of European Jewry.³⁶ In 1943, the genocide of the Jews appeared to Hannah Arendt as a rupture of history, 'something that should never have happened'.³⁷ In exile and 'without a world', she was at this time one of the rare observers of European events capable of reacting as a true 'citizen of the world'. Her articles published in *Aufbau*, *Partisan Review* and other New York periodicals of the years 1940–45 are striking evidence of this.

Totalitarianism

It was in New York, where she arrived in 1941 after fleeing from Nazified Europe, that Arendt wrote *The Origins of Totalitarianism*. This work, which took shape over a whole decade, between the Second World War and the Cold War, completed a reflection begun in 1933: if the pariah was the person who has no right to a political existence, his destiny prefigures the condition of humanity under totalitarianism, which corresponds, according to Arendt, to the world generated by the destruction of the political sphere. Totalitarianism is the radical suppression of the public sphere, conceived as an open space of interaction of distinct political subjects, the expression of pluralism. Its aim is the creation of a monolithic community without internal divisions, the negation of any form of alterity: the stateless are its first victims. As well as political enemies of the regime, concentration camps receive religious, ethnic or social minorities considered irreducible to the reshaping of society into a homogeneous community. The death camps were reserved for Jews, and to a lesser degree for Gypsies, the most emblematic embodiments of the pariah: 'The Nazis started their extermination of Jews by first depriving them of all legal status... and before they set the gas chambers into motion they had carefully tested the ground and found out to their satisfaction that no country would claim these people. The point is that a condition of complete rightlessness was created before the right to life was challenged.'³⁸

In a text of the 1950s, Arendt rejected ontological conceptions of politics, defining this as the domain of the *infra*, an expression not of being but of the relationship between human beings ('the space that is *between* men'), thus implying their diversity.³⁹ We can note in this definition traces of Heidegger's view of being as 'being-with' (*Mitsein*), in other words, as plurality of the world.⁴⁰ As distinct from the author of *Sein und Zeit*, however, for whom this proved the inauthenticity of being 'cast' into the world, for Arendt on the contrary it was the indispensable premise of politics, conceived as construction of a common world. Totalitarianism was the antithesis of the 'being-in-community' that found its accomplishment in a shared public sphere.

The unclassifiable character of a work like *The Origins of Totalitarianism* – neither a Marxist theory of fascism, nor a liberal theory of despotism, nor again a sociology of power after the functionalist models then fashionable in the United States – was the reason for an incomprehension that formed an obstacle to its reception for several decades. The title certainly contributed to this problem, at a time – the early years of the Cold War – when the concept of totalitarianism was solidly rooted in the Western camp. It was inevitable, in fact, that when anti-totalitarianism became synonymous with anti-communism Arendt's book was interpreted as a 'bible of the Cold War' and placed on the *index librorum proibitorum* of a left submitted to Stalinist hegemony. Arendt's desire to think politics beyond – if not against – classical schemas, without making a choice between right and left, contributed to increasing the misunderstanding. Her ambiguous relationship with the Congress for Cultural Freedom, with which she collaborated despite attacking it in her private letters and viewing certain of its members as corrupt individuals to be shunned, did not help either to clarify her position.[41] It is true that, once she had obtained American citizenship, she did not hesitate to denounce McCarthyism and arouse public opinion against those ex-communists who had become Cold War warriors, whom she was careful to distinguish from 'former Communists'.[42] In London, at the same time, Isaac Deutscher distinguished between 'heretics' and 'renegades' (communists who became anti-Stalinist and those who became anti-communist), in a definition that sought not to cast anathemas but rather to describe a psychological attitude and a mental habitus.[43] Arendt escaped this dichotomy. In a world divided into hostile blocs, however, her position appeared incomprehensible and encountered a certain distrust. During the 1950s, when the reception of her writings was more or less confined to America and Germany, the misunderstanding was total.

It took time to understand that *The Origins of Totalitarianism* is in reality a radical questioning of the history of the West. Written in haste during the war, on the basis of a documentation that was partial and insufficient, the book today shows its limits. Nazism and Stalinism are juxtaposed rather than compared; the difference between concentration camps and extermination camps is never made clear; the relationship between Soviet communism, anti-Semitism and imperialism is not explained and remains problematic. It remains, however, that as distinct from liberal interpretations, for which totalitarianism is a threat to Western civilization, Arendt interprets it as one of Western civilization's most authentic products, its premises being anti-Semitism and imperialism. Modern anti-Semitism was no longer the old religious Judeophobia, but a racial hatred that made Jews the scapegoat for the crisis of the Old World. The 'Jewish question' illustrates the collapse of a continental order based on a model – the nation-state – that was unable to disassociate citizenship from ethnos and became an actual factory of statelessness. Arendt therefore viewed totalitarianism as the ironic revenge of Edmund Burke.[44] The merciless critic of the French Revolution was not wrong after all in denouncing the mystifying character of the philosophy of human rights, which postulated an abstract humanity to which it ideally attributed a set of 'natural rights' that, in reality, only states are in a position to grant their members. Finally, imperialism was the laboratory of a new relationship between ideology (racism conceived as science) and terror (the 'administrative massacres'[45] of the colonial world). At a time when the concept of totalitarianism had established itself in political science as a weapon of the 'free world' against its enemies,[46] Arendt developed a theory of totalitarianism that was a radical critique of the West, seeing it as the epilogue to an age-old tradition of domination and oppression.

Paradoxically, the misunderstanding that accompanied the success of her book in the 1950s had the same roots as the silence that surrounded other works of German-Jewish exile in these years, such as Horkheimer and Adorno's *Dialectic of Reason* (1947) or Walter Benjamin's 'Theses on the Concept of History' (1940). After the defeat of Nazism, communists identified the USSR with civilization and progress, while liberals defended the 'free world', heir to Western values, against the threat embodied by totalitarian communism.[47] When the defeat of Nazism was celebrated as a new triumph of the Enlightenment, no one was prepared to see totalitarianism as a product of Western civilization and a paroxysmic expression of its own contradictions. Only a few were able to grasp Hannah Arendt's most fertile intuitions. The genetic relationship that linked Nazism to imperialism and nineteenth-century colonialism remains still today a historical workshop largely unexplored.

Memory and justice

Ten years later, Arendt's famous essay *Eichmann in Jerusalem* (1963) gave rise to another misunderstanding that soon developed into a ferocious polemic. In the context of the time, the book's subtitle – 'A report on the banality of evil' – was perceived as an insufferable provocation.[48] With a half century of hindsight, it is clear today that the 'banality' that Arendt speaks of refers to the executioner, not to the crime of which he was accused. What was 'banal' in her eyes was not the extermination of the Jews but the personality of Eichmann. The worst crimes in the history of humanity can be perpetrated by ordinary individuals, in this instance obtuse bureaucrats, neither fanatics nor bedevilled by hatred, but unable to think and thus understand what they do. When the book appeared, however, the majority of commentators interpreted the subtitle as an attempt to banalize the Holocaust. Some even saw it as an apology for Nazism (*Le Nouvel Observateur* even had the front-page headline 'Is Hannah Arendt a Nazi?'). Others broke off all relations with her, like her Zionist friends Kurt Blumenfeld and Gershom Scholem, following a tense and tormented dialogue that revealed incompatibilities of language and approach. What lay behind this imbroglio? The essential reason probably lies in the wide gap between Arendt's reflections, which took the measure of the Shoah already during the war, and international opinion – including Jewish – for which this trial was a traumatic moment of amnesia, the start of a work of mourning that had not taken place in 1945. In Jerusalem, Arendt had her eyes fixed on Eichmann, scrutinizing his personality, seeking to penetrate his psychology, culture, motivations, mentality. For international opinion, the trial was that of Nazism as responsible for the Holocaust, the trial that had not taken place in Nuremberg at the end of the war. Now 50 years after its publication, Arendt's book has become a classic. Today we can find in it the premises for a functionalist interpretation of Nazism, very widespread in the 1980s and 1990s, that saw the Shoah as a bureaucratic, administrative, industrial extermination, carried out by an anonymous and impersonal machine. Arendt's reading has almost become normative, to the point of forgetting the 'Shoah by bullets'. We are now beginning to understand the extermination of the Jews as a singular synthesis of 'hot' and 'cold' violence, of eruption of hatred and elimination by technical mechanisms, of 'de-civilizing' (the fall of the moral and psychological barriers obstructing recourse to violence) and 'civilization' (the instrumental rationality and technical apparatuses of the modern world).

After the publication of *Eichmann in Jerusalem*, the break between Arendt and Scholem deepened to the point of being irreversible. Their exchange of letters is interesting, as it casts light on Arendt's relationship to Jewishness and, indirectly, her conception of politics. Considering the notion of 'banality of evil' simply an unpleasant and inappropriate slogan, Scholem accused his old friend – they had met through Walter Benjamin in the 1930s – of 'heartlessness' (*Herzlosigkeit*) and absence of 'love of the Jewish people' (*Ahavat Israel*).[49] In other words, he reproached her for her lack of empathy for the victims. In her reply, Arendt admitted having abandoned the Kantian concept of 'radical evil' (*radikale Böse*) that she had used in her previous work on totalitarianism. The notion of 'radical evil' denoted an evil that had roots and motivation, that expressed a maleficent intention, whereas the Eichmann trial had revealed to her the existence of an evil that was extreme and invasive but not radical, that is, lacking depth or demoniacal dimension. Eichmann seemed to her the embodiment of a 'new type of criminal', for whom it had become impossible to distinguish between good and evil, and who could thus perpetrate monstrous crimes without being conscious of this. His organizational and administrative talents in a criminal activity were accompanied by an astonishing 'inability to think'.[50] As she wrote to Karl Jaspers during the trial, this banality of evil is 'something that cannot even be adequately represented either in legal terms or in political terms'.[51] And this 'inability to think' is precisely one of the features of totalitarian domination, destructive of politics and incompatible with individual autonomy. As for her supposed lack of 'love for the Jewish people', she acknowledged without hesitation how such a sentiment was foreign to her, perceiving it as the expression of a turn of mind that she had always fought against. Though her Jewishness was beyond doubt, this was not the result of an inner substance, whether religious or moral, but rather of a historical condition bound up with persecution (under Nazism, she wrote in 1959, denying her Jewishness would have been 'a grotesque and dangerous evasion of reality').[52] She viewed Jewishness as the source of her independence of mind (Lessing's *Selbstdenken*),[53] not as a religious or community allegiance. Finally, the correspondence between Scholem and Arendt makes explicit two opposing approaches to the Eichmann trial. In Israel this was seen as the trial of anti-Semitism by Zionism. Scholem accepted this logic, whereas Arendt saw the Shoah as a crime against humanity, which happened to be embodied by the Jews. She did not deny the legitimacy of the Israeli court, but believed that an international criminal court – which did not exist at this time – would have been more appropriate to judge such a crime, since Israeli justice could not pronounce a verdict in the name of all the victims.[54]

The public sphere

In 1951, the year in which her *Origins of Totalitarianism* was published, Hannah Arendt obtained United States citizenship. The 'dark times' were over. Officially, she was no longer a stateless exile. Her naturalization coincided with the success of her book and the start of a brilliant academic career that led her for some 20 years to teach in the most prestigious American universities, from the anti-conformist New School of Social Research in New York to the very respectable University of Chicago, where political philosophy was dominated by the austere figure of Leo Strauss. In this period, the notion of 'stateless' no longer denoted, in her writings, a condition of the present, but rather a characteristic of Jewish historical experience. A new stage then opened, in which it was no longer totalitarianism that occupied the central place in her thought, but rather what totalitarianism sought to destroy: the public sphere. More precisely, Arendt rethought a set of concepts such as 'action', 'freedom' and 'plurality', which acquired their meaning only when inscribed in such a public sphere. A series of books thus appeared – in particular *The Human Condition* (1958) and *On Revolution* (1963) – that renewed postwar political theory and, in a certain sense, enabled Arendt to find a point of anchorage. Neither left nor right, neither Marxist nor liberal, neither progressive nor conservative, at least according to classic schemas, Arendt's thought found a refuge in the tradition of republicanism, based on a view of politics as participation and the civic virtue of action aiming at the common good. From the nineteenth century, this tradition had been shaken by the rise of socialism and the advent of the modern cleavage between left and right. Arendt renewed republicanism by going beyond its rifts, and thus generated new ambiguities.

This turn in Arendt's thought, moreover, formed part of a wider metamorphosis of the German-Jewish exiles in the United States, which we analysed in the second chapter of this book: the transition from *Bildung* to the Bill of Rights. Excluded by definition from the German *Volk*, and accepted as citizens by a state of Christian origin that continued to inflict on them many forms of political discrimination, German Jews had built throughout the nineteenth century an identity founded on culture. To be German meant first and foremost having access to German culture, and the path of this cultural assimilation was *Bildung*, the ideal of education and self-improvement set by Humboldt in the age of *Aufklärung*.[55] In the United States, German Jews had discovered a multi-ethnic and multicultural nation in which being American meant adhering to the Constitution. Brought up in the cult of Goethe, and educated in the school of Heideggerian existentialism, in the United States Arendt came to know an Atlantic tradition based on notions of liberty, law, norms, pluralism and public debate. Certain pages of her correspondence reflect this discovery. In a letter to Jaspers of 1946, she writes of how she finally had a concrete idea of what it meant to live in a society in which the national antagonisms that had torn apart and almost submerged Europe were unknown:

> There is much I could say about America. There really is such a thing as freedom here and a strong feeling among many people that one cannot live without freedom. The republic is not a vapid illusion, and the fact that there is no national state and no truly national tradition creates an atmosphere of freedom or at least one not pervaded by fanaticism... Then, too, people here feel themselves responsible for public life to an extent I have never seen in any European country.[56]

Arendt revisited the Atlantic tradition in the light of classical Greek philosophy, a process that led her to insist on the participative dimension of politics. As against the liberal view of 'negative liberty', based on the valorization of individual rights involving the private sphere, and particularly property, Arendt saw liberty as the autonomy of equal subjects interacting in a public space by way of collective deliberation. This public space, Arendt explained, 'means, first, that everything that appears in public can be seen and heard by everybody and has the widest possible publicity'.[57] This 'ocular' or 'agonal' interpretation of politics, in the definition that Seyla Benhabib gives of it,[58] is what is singular to Arendt's view of the public sphere, distinguishing it for example from that of Jürgen Habermas, who is less sensitive to participation and more oriented to the activity of communication.[59] This is why Benhabib calls Arendt's a 'reluctant' modernism. It is clear that this rediscovery of the liberty of antiquity – direct democracy – presents libertarian features, and this explains Arendt's keen interest in the experience of workers' councils – not in the Soviet form of 1917 but rather the Hungarian experience of 1956 – as well as her enthusiasm for Rosa Luxemburg, or again her sympathy for the barricades of May 1968.[60] Based on an 'agonal' conception of action, Arendt's republicanism shows a great distrust of any kind of political representation, thus accentuating the libertarian dimension of her thought while distancing it from partisan commitment.

The commodity reification of the public sphere and the decline in the legislative power – in a world where information belongs to the great communications monopolies and where parliaments simply ratify laws elaborated by the executive power, giving rise to a kind of permanent state of exception – give Arendt's political theory anti-conformist or even subversive features. But this still does not remove its limits and contradictions. Arendt describes 'action' as a domain of liberty that presupposes emancipation from needs, transcending both the sphere of reproduction of life ('labour') and that of material creation ('work').[61] But she does not indicate how to construct this reign of liberty. In her eyes, the path to follow is not that of social emancipation, as she explains in her essay on revolution, in which, echoing Burke – and this time without irony[62] – she contrasts the American Revolution, aiming at liberty, with the French Revolution, ineluctably drifting towards despotism because of its quest for the 'happiness of the people'.[63] Reviewing Arendt's essay, Eric Hobsbawm does not hide his sceptical amazement in the face of a 'metaphysical and normative' conception of revolution analysed as a de-historicized phenomenon and deprived of a social subject.⁶⁴ Because of this radical opposition between the principle of liberty and the desire for social emancipation, Arendt's republicanism ends up with a conception of the autonomy of politics in which certain commentators have seen an existentialist accent, as a kind of return to origins.⁶⁵

This then seems the fundamental limit of a political theory developed from a particular observatory, that of prosperous postwar America, and through a prism that was quite specific, that of the Jewish question in Europe of the first half of the twentieth century. This limit lies in the inability to see (or the refusal to admit) the social dimension of oppression. Having rejected the idea of social emancipation as politically dangerous, and at the same time dismissed the classic liberal view in which the market offers a natural solution to social conflicts, Arendt took refuge in an abstract and disembodied republicanism. A liberal such as Benjamin Constant was not wrong in recalling that the liberty of antiquity depended on slavery. Hannah Arendt clings to a conception of liberty that underestimates the commodity reification of the public sphere and deliberately excludes any idea of social citizenship. In other words, she seems to ignore the fact that political participation presupposes access to culture and information, mastery of the tools of reflection, a certain availability of time and, above all, the satisfaction of socially determined needs. When, in the late 1950s, she tried to transpose the Jewish prism to the interpretation of the Black question in the United States, the result left many of her readers perplexed. Asserting that the problem had been resolved by the elimination of segregationist laws, and that it would be harmful to try and go any further, Arendt advanced the idea that once the legal ghetto was eliminated, the survival of social ghettos was basically legitimate: 'The question is not how to abolish discrimination, but how to keep it confined within the social sphere, where it is legitimate, and prevent its trespassing on the political and the personal sphere, where it is destructive.'⁶⁶

A concept of action and the public sphere born out of reflection on the Jewish question in the twentieth century – the deprivation of rights and the persecution that struck a minority social integrated for more than a century – could not grasp the deep imbrication of political discrimination, racial stigmatization and social oppression that lay at the heart of the Black question in the United States. Arendt's choice of 'taking her historical and political orientation on the basis of the Jewish question' enabled her to find some decisive keys to interpreting the twentieth century, but at the same time it blocked off other perspectives. The Jewish prism is not generalizable.

This singular osmosis between libertarian aspirations and a stubborn refusal to see social oppression is perhaps the key to explaining the posthumous canonization of Hannah Arendt in European culture from the 1980s on, when her writings became an emergency exit for a generation of intellectuals rendered spiritually 'homeless', orphans of Marxism but not yet ready to espouse classical liberalism. The collapse of communism and the emergence of the memory of the Shoah helped the definitive (if belated) rehabilitation of the theoretician of totalitarianism and the killjoy of the Eichmann trial. Jewish, exiled, a woman, a philosopher, a brilliant essayist, a libertarian and unsubmissive mind, disciple and then lover of a major German thinker who compromised with Nazism, Hannah Arendt came to exert an irresistible power of fascination, to the point of being transformed into an icon of twentieth-century culture. Not only has her work acquired the classic status that it deserves, it has also become a cultural fashion. There can be no doubt, for anyone with a minimal familiarity with her correspondence, that she would have been the first to smile at such a posthumous fate, quite unexpected for someone who had discovered politics through becoming aware of her pariah status.

5
Metamorphoses: From Judeophobia to Islamophobia

As we have seen, the end of Jewish modernity was a product of the cataclysms of the twentieth century. Far from being the result of an endogenous process, a kind of natural exhaustion of which it would be sufficient to detect and study the sources, it was a direct consequence of the transformations that affected all Western societies. In other words, it was the product of a global history that involves but goes beyond the Jews, actors in their history – to use the classic formula – in the context of circumstances that they did not choose and could often neither control nor steer. The entire trajectory of this modernity was an encounter between Jews and the surrounding world, in a complex dialectic between emancipation and anti-Semitism. One of the reasons for the end of Jewish modernity lies precisely in the end of this dialectic, in a world in which recognition was no longer an objective to pursue, and anti-Semitism had completely lost any respectability. If the decline of anti-Semitism formed an essential premise for this metamorphosis, we need to study the forms that this took – was it a mere exhaustion or was it replaced by other forms of exclusion? – and also its consequences.

The decline of anti-Semitism

Born in the late eighteenth century, then developing in symbiosis with colonialism and nationalism, modern racism reached its apogee in the last century, when the combination of fascism and anti-Semitism had an exterminatory epilogue in Nazi Germany. Once this abscess had been burst, after the Second World War – as we saw in the first chapter – anti-Semitism underwent a decline, while racism metamorphosed, abandoning its hierarchical and 'racialist' orientation (in the old model of Gobineau, Chamberlain, Vacher de Lapouge or Lombroso) and becoming differentialist and culturalist. In other words, it slipped from 'racial science' into ethnocentrism.[1] We sometimes get the impression, from reading certain commentators in the media, that Europe is threatened by a new wave of anti-Jewish hatred, as if the old demons temporarily appeased had suddenly reawakened and were active once more. But this impression is deceptive. There is a great confusion in this debate, in which perfectly well-founded concerns mingle with basic misapprehensions, and the temptation to interpret new phenomena in old categories is ever-present. Basically, when the insurmountable traumas bequeathed by the past are projected onto the present, debate slips into polemics that are both virulent and sterile.

The phenomenon of course is real. Despite often being approximate, deceptive or based on debatable criteria, opinion polls and statistics indicate the persistence of Judeophobia in several countries. From arson attacks on synagogues, schools and Israelite communities, to murders tinged with hatred – particularly in France – not forgetting the threatening declarations of the former Iranian president Mahmoud Ahmadinejad, these repeated acts cannot be viewed as isolated or insignificant.[2] There is a current tendency, however, to group them together despite their differences in a single homogeneous, universal and timeless category: anti-Semitism, seen as the normal and constant modality of relations between Jews and gentiles. The effort to understand thus gives way to confusion, with a tendency to include phenomena of different natures: religious anti-Judaism, Enlightenment atheism, racist anti-Semitism, left- or right-wing anti-Zionism, and finally criticism of Israeli policy, are systematically reduced to a single matrix, of which they are supposedly only outward expressions of a long and uninterrupted history. Luther, Voltaire, Drumont, Hitler and Arafat, and today Ahmadinejad, thus become masks for a hatred against Jews that is always the same. This approach has inspired a wide literature – Léon Poliakov's *Histoire de l'antisémitisme* is the most interesting example – and has gradually become a kind of habitus for several observers.[3] And yet this is the least pertinent way of deciphering the present situation. In order to avoid hasty and deceptive reduction, certain distinctions are indispensable between classic anti-Semitism and the new Judeophobias, between anti-Semitism and anti-Zionism. These are no more than elementary precautions, without which understanding of the past is impossible and its public use can only give rise to misunderstandings.

In the wake of Pierre-André Taguieff, who distinguishes *racialism* (the idea of races as the motor of history) from *racism* (a prejudice giving rise to practices), we can separate ideological anti-Semitism – the golden age of which ran from the late nineteenth century to the Second World War, from Drumont to Hitler – from anti-Semitism as a diffuse prejudice, the source of a more or less declared hostility, not necessarily bound up with discriminatory practices, of which some vestiges still persist today. In the late nineteenth century, Jews were perceived as elements foreign to the nation, its traditions, its culture and even its psychology, rootless and enemies of the most authentic values. In France, Captain Dreyfus embodied this equation between Jews, foreigners and republic. The anti-Dreyfusard campaign became a conservative and anti-Semitic challenge to the 'Jewish republic'. Anti-Semitism could take specific forms in different national contexts – pogroms and trials for ritual murder in the Russian empire, *völkisch* nationalism in Germany and Austria, anti-republican conservatism in France, Catholic anti-liberalism in Italy – but they shared the same view of the Jew as metaphor of modernity. The anti-Jewish tirades of the Jesuits of Civiltà cattolica did not draw on the same sources as the cultural pessimism of someone like Paul Lagarde; the synthesis of racism, anti-capitalism and anti-Judaism to be found in Édouard Drumont's *La France juive* did not have the same scientific pretensions as the eugenicist anti-Semitism of the social anthropologist Georges Vacher de Lapouge or a Nazi ideologue such as Hans Günther; yet they all identified the Jews with a detested modern civilization. This kind of anti-Semitism has long since ceased to provoke moral indignation or even arouse criticism, being so far away from today's sensibilities; it strikes us today as an aberration, a strange and curious phenomenon, in the same way as the 'human zoos' that were so popular with the European public until the 1930s.

Anti-Semitism as prejudice and social practice, however, remains, yet it is the object of a general condemnation both in civil society and in state institutions. Its manifestations are residual. The writer Renaud Camus, who sprinkles the pages of his diaries with allusions to Jews as intruders in French culture, acting in it as a foreign body, belong to an old tradition that goes back to Drumont, Maurras and Bloy.[4] The cartoonist Forattini, when he depicted in the Italian newspaper *La Stampa* the Israeli occupation of Bethlehem with the baby Jesus once more crucified by the Jews, conveyed a fantasy – ritual murder – that has weighed for millennia on the Christian imagination.[5] And a trace of this age-old prejudice remains in the well-known aphorism according to which, if the Jews were exterminated, they must have somehow been to blame (as the historian and ex-diplomat Sergio Romano could still write in a recent essay).[6] When Martin Walser calls on his fellow-Germans to no longer live in the shadow of the Holocaust and rediscover their national pride, he gives voice to an anti-Semitism that is more deeply rooted than is apparent in the public sphere, the anti-Semitism of those who see Jews as Germany's eternal 'misfortune' (*die Juden sind unser Unglück*, wrote the historian Heinrich von Treitschke in 1879).[7]

This anti-Semitism must not be trivialized, yet neither should its impact be overestimated. It is simply a residue, the survival of a phenomenon whose decline is apparent, if analysed over the *longue durée*, and which does not seem to affect younger generations. Its manifestations are limited, episodic and arouse scandal precisely because they come up against a widely diffused sensibility that no longer accepts this prejudice. Anti-Semitic language, which until the Second World War was deep-rooted, virulent and yet accepted as respectable, has lost all legitimacy. This shift took place in the wake of the Holocaust, a turning-point that broke the continuity of both European history and anti-Semitism. The integration of the Shoah into Europe's historical awareness made this discourse intolerable. Anti-Semitism is no longer acceptable in the nationalist and conservative right-wing parties that were its guardians for so long.

In Germany, the least anti-Semitic allusion seriously endangers any political career. In Italy, Gianfranco Fini, the ex-fascist who became president of the National Assembly, completed his liberal shift in Israel with a visit to Yad Vashem, his head covered by a kippa.[8] In France, the Dominic Strauss-Kahn affair, which received planetary media coverage in 2011, was a revelatory sign of the decline of anti-Semitism. Here was one of the most powerful men in the world, head of the planet's leading financial institution, the International Monetary Fund (IMF), from a family full of both rabbis and freemasons, married to a well-known journalist, herself Jewish, from a rich family of art dealers. An ex-minister, cosmopolitan statesman who spoke with ease in several languages and was a familiar figure on the international stage, leader of the Socialist Party and likely future candidate in the presidential elections. He was suddenly caught up in a sexual scandal, first of all accused of rape by a chambermaid in a New York luxury hotel, then involved in allegations of prostitution; his sexual obsessions and connections with pimps were broadcast by the media across the world. Arrested in New York, he rented a top-end apartment and hired lawyers, again Jews, who were skilled in defending the powerful and known for their exorbitant fees. The Strauss-Kahn affair concentrated all the ingredients susceptible of arousing an old mythology, and there can be no doubt that, in another age, it would have unleashed the anti-Semitic press. One need only imagine the portrait of such a character that would have been penned by Édouard Drumont or Léon Daudet, by the pencils of Toulouse-Lautrec or the crayons of Caran d'Ache. Or even what someone like Pierre Poujade would have said in the 1950s, given his tirades against Pierre Mendès-France and his 'anti-Gaulois' spirit.[9] Yet there was nothing of the kind. It was almost impossible to detect, in the rivers of ink devoted to Dominic Strauss-Kahn, the least anti-Semitic allusion. If his Jewishness was frequently mentioned, it was never offered by way of explanation, evidence or confirmation of his morally reprehensible actions. None of his political opponents, neither on the left nor on the right, even the xenophobic far right, deemed it useful to exploit this scandal with arguments drawn from the old anti-Semitic arsenal.[10] Everyone, even the most cynical, feared that by using these they would only discredit themselves. And that is perfectly true. On this point at least, even one of the most deplorable cases in recent public life proved to be a comforting test.

The main version of postwar anti-Semitism, negationism – the idea that the Holocaust was a myth, a new Jewish plot aiming to blame the Gentiles[11] – has survived as a provocative and transgressive discourse that has met with general condemnation and often led to prosecution (leading to advantage being taken of the 'victim' stance that this creates). The fact that, after having been ignored or repressed for decades, the memory of the Holocaust has been transformed today into a kind of civil religion in the Western world, sometimes protected by the law, shows the profound isolation of anti-Semitic discourse and ideas.

The new Judeophobia

The Israeli-Palestinian conflict gave rise to a 'left' anti-Semitism, which must be condemned but remains the phenomenon of a small minority, incomparable with the gusts of anti-Jewish fever that periodically swept the workers' and socialist movements, particularly in France, from the early nineteenth century to the 1930s.[12] It has also generated a new Judeophobia that is widespread in the Islamic world (and among its minorities in Europe), which sometimes gives rise to acts of anti-Semitism. The very widespread distribution in Arabic of the anti-Semitic classic *Protocols of the Elders of Zion* is a clear enough symptom of this tendency, as well as the expressions mentioned above. To set fire to a synagogue is an anti-Semitic act that must be condemned and punished, but it is useful to grasp its motivations if one wishes to combat it. Those young people of Maghreb or sub-Saharan origin from the poorest suburbs who carry out acts of this kind – small minorities yet enjoying a complacent regard if not tacit approval from wider layers – are expressing a system of values and a cultural universe very different from those that formerly fed European anti-Semitism. They make Jews a scapegoat for their suffering, thus transforming them into a metaphorical figure for many converging sentiments (and resentments). Jews are identified with the elite of a system that has always excluded and oppressed them, not just in the suburbs where the police are the only visible presence of the state, but also in Iraq, Afghanistan or the Palestinian territories occupied by Israel. Old anti-Semitic stereotypes – in particular the equation of the Jews with money – can easily be grafted on to this confused substratum of sentiments and beliefs, with an amplifying and distorting effect. When this state of abandonment and exclusion leads to delinquency, the result is the monstrous phenomenon of a criminality with anti-Semitic coloration. In recent years France has been the theatre of this, with several murders that have been widely reported. A horrific killing of the young Ilan Halimi, in February 2006, was one of its most serious episodes. According to the outcome of the trial, his murderers – a gang of self-proclaimed 'barbarians' that specialized in kidnapping – chose him because their leader, Youssef Fofana, was convinced that 'a Jew must be rich'.[13] This anti-Semitism took on an explicitly political dimension with the case of Mohamed Merah, the young

Frenchman who in March 2012 killed in cold blood a schoolteacher and three children in the courtyard of a Jewish school in Toulouse. In conversations with the police who encircled his apartment, during the interminable siege that preceded his elimination, Merah explained his motivations: 'I killed Jewish children because my Muslim little brothers and sisters are getting killed... I kill Jews in France because those same Jews... are killing innocent people in Palestine.'[14] Here we have horrific crimes and crazy statements that cannot be classified in the long list of anti-Jewish exclusion and persecution, as these are phenomena that often affect the perpetrators themselves, and these criminal acts are precisely how they react. This fact certainly does not lessen such crimes; it only makes them the more tragic, and demands an explanation beyond horror and condemnation.

This hatred of the Jews, writes Michel Wieviorka, 'arises from a logic of the ghetto, a combination of social exclusion and racist discrimination' accentuated by 'a deep sense of being rejected and trapped in a place of relegation'.[15] There is a striking historical paradox, this sociologist observes, in this turn that identifies Jews with an oppression that they have themselves suffered, and of which they are the historical symbol, but the paradox is precisely evidence of the great change in a world where Jews no longer form an oppressed minority. The memory of the Shoah, cultivated by a state that constructs urban ghettos, risks having effects quite contrary to its supposed pedagogic virtues.

This then is the background to the new Judeophobia, in which Islamic fundamentalism inserts itself in an attempt to give it a political dimension. To recognize that this Judeophobia arises from a legitimate revolt against a very real oppression does not mean justifying it, as history teaches us that rebellion can also take a false orientation, sterile or harmful. To confound the United States imperial policy, Israel, the West, the Jews and their synagogues into a single bloc is not only an act of ignorance or cultural backwardness (which also explains the vote for the far right on the part of underprivileged social strata with low 'cultural capital'), it is above all the result of a political regression whose causes are multiple and widely shared. The degraded social fabric of the suburbs does not explain everything. The young Arabs who organized the march for equality in 1983 were in many cases born in the shantytowns that appeared in France at the time of the Algerian war. What changed, between 1983 and the revolt of 2005, between the struggle for equality and the burning of cars, was the political context. Behind this Judeophobia – in parallel with the spread of political Islam – lies the defeat of all the ideologies born of decolonization, from nationalism to pan-Arabism, anti-imperialism to socialism. Frantz Fanon seems to have made way for Osama Bin Laden; if the latter has been killed, the former has not made a return, except for a minority of postcolonial intellectuals. There has subsequently been the incapacity of the western European democracies to integrate the generations born from the postcolonial wave of immigration, who remain excluded and marginalized. This failure reveals the aporias of a universalism that postulates equality in the form of assimilation to a normative model – the nation-state – but stigmatizes ethnic, religious and cultural alterities. And there has also been another defeat, that of internationalism. Within the European left, representatives of so-called 'visible' minorities, names with an Arabic, Asiatic or African sound, remain rare. There are millions of immigrants of postcolonial origin or their descendants in Europe today, but they have scant public visibility outside of sporting competitions and a few artists and writers. By a strange coincidence, this marginalization has been effected in parallel with the acquisition of a new respectability by Jews. It is against this background that the new Judeophobia has arisen. Its target is a minority, which, after having historically embodied a figure of alterity in the Western world, has today become the symbol of this.

We must add that the remedies so far tried have been counter-productive. In the years that followed the attacks of 11 September 2001, Islamic fundamentalism was fuelled by a racist campaign that sought to present every young Muslim as a potential terrorist. This Eurocentric propensity, the expression of an ill-digested colonial past, can also take the form of an intransigent defence of the secular and republican tradition, as has happened in several countries with the promulgation of laws that, on the pretext of forbidding any 'ostensible sign of religious adherence' in the public space, actually aim at stigmatizing one particular minority. As well as this, confusion is deliberately fostered by the spokespeople for religious communities that, while claiming to represent Jews as a whole, proclaim an unconditional support for Israel. This total identification with Israel ultimately promotes the negative equation that leads anti-Semites to profane a synagogue seen as an expression of the 'Jewish state'.[16] After the first round of the French presidential election of 2002, Roger Cukiermann, head of the Conseil Représentatif des Institurions juives de France (CRIF), greeted the success of the Front National candidate as a salutary warning to the Islamists.[17]

Anti-Semitism and anti-Zionism

Here we must dwell for a moment on the hasty assimilation of anti-Zionism to anti-Semitism. In France, such people as Pierre-André Taguieff, otherwise a more inspired historian of political thought, the essayist Pascal Bruckner, the political analyst Alexandre Adler and others have deliberately lent themselves to this game, with a pronounced taste for syncretism, coining such new notions as 'Islamo-fascism' and 'Islamo-leftism', hollow yet resonant, and above all interchangeable.[18] Anti-Zionist Jews or those critical of Israeli policy do not escape this criticism, and find themselves accused of being 'Jewish traitors... infinitely more despicable, infinitely more repugnant' than the everyday anti-Semite.[19]

Anti-Zionism can indeed conceal anti-Semitism, but Zionism is certainly not above suspicion. Historically, it had its own fascist tendencies. In the 1930s, the Mufti of Jerusalem, Amin al-Husseini's admiration for fascism was shared by the 'revisionist' Zionist Vladimir Zeev Jabotinsky, whose followers paraded in uniform.[20] With both of these, it was a case of ideological borrowings. Nazi anti-Semitism offered the former an argument justifying his pan-Islamist anti-Judaism, while fascism offered the latter the model of a radical nationalism. The one wanted an Islamist Palestine without Jews, the other a Jewish Palestine without Arabs.

Over the years, an emotional and almost 'religious' tie to Israel has developed within the Jewish diaspora, somewhat reminiscent of the myth of the USSR cultivated by European communists in Stalin's time. The USSR was above all criticism, and those who dared to express doubts about its policies were automatically denounced as anti-communists, warmongers and accomplices of US imperialism. By similar criteria, an inflexible opponent of Israel's occupation of Lebanon such as Primo Levi, who in 1982 referred to Begin as a 'fascist',[21] would today risk being classed among the anti-Semites. The identification of anti-Zionism with anti-Semitism is the trick that makes it possible to automatically neutralize any criticism of Israeli policy. After 11 September 2001, Claude Lanzmann published an article on the front page of *Le Monde* in which he called those opposing the war on Afghanistan anti-Semites and accused them of a secret desire to bomb Israel.[22] This is the inevitable consequence of a very widespread attitude that consists of de-historicizing and de-contextualizing the Israeli-Palestinian conflict and transforming it into a 'clash of civilizations', an irreducible antagonism between opposing 'essences': Jews and Muslims, Jews and anti-Semites, the West and the Islamic world, etc.[23]

Unfortunately, this reflex is not simply the work of demagogy and instrumentalization. It also plays on old fears and resentments accumulated over time. It follows from a wounded memory, a trauma that was repressed and hidden for a long while. It is not hard to grasp the fantastic dimension of these representations. The Israeli-Palestinian conflict has become the object of interpretations that transcend its context to the point of transforming it into a screen on which many other concerns, rancours and moments of memory are projected. In Europe, the debate on anti-Semitism is fuelled by the Middle East crisis, but its real object remains the Holocaust, whose shadow still weighs on the present. Collective memory is neither immobile nor immutable, and above all it is always exposed to the risk of excess and abuse. It can become a distorting prism through which reality is deciphered, by transposing categories born in one context into another completely different one. Twenty years ago, the first Iraq war was transformed into a kind of 'war of memories', in which real actors played the role of intermediaries in a settling of accounts with the past.[24] Saddam Hussein was depicted as a new Hitler – so Bush senior defined him – while opponents of the Western crusade were cast a posteriori as his accomplices preparing to perpetrate a new genocide.

This phenomenon took on its most extreme forms in France, among turncoats from the left (often Jewish) who transformed themselves into bitter champions of neoconservatism (well deserving the nickname of '*maorrassiens*' or '*maoccidents*'),[25] and in Germany, the birthplace over the last two decades of a left that is radically 'anti-German' (*antideutsch*) and pro-Israeli. Faced with the legacy of their past, still not always clear, and their historical misunderstanding of the nature of Nazi anti-Semitism, these currents react by a kind of outbidding, making the defence of Israel a real dogma. For some of them, Israel is still threatened by a Europe desirous of perpetuating the anti-Semitism of the Enlightenment (a project of eradicating Jewish alterity that culminated in the Shoah).[26] A journal such as *Konkret*, which supported Palestine Liberation Organization (PLO) terrorism at a time when the organization did not recognize Israel, today defends the occupation of Palestinian territories.[27]

Postfascism

The decline of traditional anti-Semitism, and the adoption of a well-wishing attitude towards Zionism, are at the heart of a mutation in the European far right movements. For the first time in history, Jews and the far right have ceased to be incompatible worlds, irreducibly opposed to one another, as they are no longer divided by anti-Semitism. Nationalists have put their anti-Semitism in parentheses, and their Islamophobia is capable of seducing a section of Jewish opinion. Racism is perpetuated by donning a new skin and adding new categories to its inexhaustible 'treasury' of exclusion and hatred.

The interweaving of racism, fascism, nationalism and anti-Semitism that occurred in Europe in the first half of the twentieth century no longer exists today. Nationalism and anti-Semitism continue to proliferate in the new East European members of the European Union, where they are able to link up with a history interrupted in 1945 and feed off resentments built up over four decades of 'real socialism'. In this part of the continent they claim their filiation with the dictatorships of the 1930s, like Jobbik in Hungary, which has taken up the legacy of the 'arrowed cross' and cultivates the memory of Admiral Horthy; they exhume an old revanchist and expansionist mythology, as with the Greater Romania Party or the Croat Party of the Right (HSP), which continues the Ustachi movement of Ante Pavelic. In western Europe, however, fascism is practically non-existent as an organized political force, at least in those countries that were its historic birthplace. In Germany, the influence of neo-Nazi movements on public opinion is almost zero. In Spain, where the legacy of Francoism was taken up by the Popular Party, national-Catholic and conservative, the Falangists are a species on the edge of extinction. In Italy, where we have seen the paradoxical phenomenon of a rehabilitation of fascism in public discourse, and even in the historical consciousness of a significant segment of the population – anti-fascism was the genetic code of the 'First Republic', not of Berlusconi's Italy – this has coincided with a profound metamorphosis of the heirs of Mussolini. Their leader Gianfranco Fini presents himself as the spokesman for a liberal, reformist and 'progressive' right. In France, though the Front National stands further to the right on the political chessboard, it has freed itself, under the impulse of Marine Le Pen, from the traditional image of a far right made up of partisans of the 'national revolution', Catholic fundamentalists and those nostalgic for Algérie française. Though it still contains a *fascisant* component, this is only a minority. At its last congress, the Front National adopted a republican rhetoric that was never previously part of its tradition. Though Marine Le Pen's succession to her father shows a desire for continuity, acquiring the features of a dynastic transition, she too shows signs of an indisputable desire for renovation: no classic fascist movement ever entrusted its leadership to a woman.

The decline in the fascist tradition, however, makes space for the rise of a new type of far right, whose ideology integrates the shifts of the twenty-first century. The cult of the strong state has given way to the critique of the welfare state, tax revolt and the championing of individual liberties.[28] The rejection of democracy – or its interpretation in a plebiscitary and authoritarian sense – does not always go together with nationalism, which in certain cases is swapped for forms of ethnocentrism that question the model of the nation-state, as shown by the Liga Nord in Italy or the Flemish far right. Elsewhere, nationalism takes the form of a defence of the West threatened by globalization and the clash of civilizations. The singular cocktail of xenophobia, individualism, defence of the rights of women and proclaimed homosexuality that Pim Fortuyn concocted in the Netherlands in 2002 was the key to a lasting electoral success. Similar features also characterize other political movements in northern Europe, such as the Vlaams Belang in Belgium, the Danish Popular Party and the Swedish far right.

Islamophobia

The element that binds this new far right together is racism, in the form of a violent rejection of immigrants. In our day, immigrants are the successor to the 'dangerous classes' of the nineteenth century, depicted by the social sciences of the time as receptacles of every social pathology, from alcoholism to criminality and prostitution, even blamed for the outbreaks of cholera.[29] These stereotypes – often condensed in a representation of the foreigner with distinctive physical and mental features – derive from an Orientalist and colonial imaginary that has always made it possible to define in negative terms uncertain and fragile identities founded on fear of the 'other', always perceived as the 'invader' and 'enemy'. In contemporary Europe, the immigrant basically has the features of the Muslim. Islamophobia plays the role for the new racism that anti-Semitism had in the past. The memory of the Shoah – a historical perception of anti-Semitism through the prism of its culmination in genocide – tends to obscure these clear analogies. The portrait of the Arab or Muslim sketched by contemporary xenophobia does not differ much from that of the Jew constructed by anti-Semitism in the early twentieth century. The beards, tefillin and kaftans of the Jewish immigrants from eastern Europe at that time correspond to the beards and veils of the Muslims of today. In both cases, the religious, cultural, clothing and dietary habits of a minority are mobilized in order to construct the negative stereotype of a foreign body that cannot be assimilated into the national community. Judaism and Islam both function as negative metaphors of alterity; a century ago, the Jew as painted by popular iconography inevitably had a hooked nose and sticking-out ears, just as Islam today is identified with the burka, despite the fact that 99.99 per cent of Muslim women living in Europe do not wear this full veil. In political terms, the spectre of Islamic terrorism has replaced that of Judeo-Bolshevism.

In this perspective, Islamophobia follows completely in the line of what we can call the anti-Jewish archive, using this term in the sense of Foucault's early writings, not for a library, a body of documents and texts, but as the regulating mode of a discursive practice: 'the law of what can be said, the system that governs the appearance of statements as unique events', 'the general system of the formation and transformation of statements'.[30] Conceived in this way, anti-Semitism is a repertoire of stereotypes, images, places, representations, stigmas and reflexes conveying a perception and a reading of the real that are condensed and codified into a stable and continuous discourse. As a discursive practice susceptible of undergoing a transfer of object, anti-Semitism has thus transmigrated into Islamophobia.

Today, anti-Semitism remains a distinctive feature of the nationalisms of eastern Europe, where Islam is almost non-existent and the turn of 1989 gave new life to the old demons (still present, even where there are no Jews), but it has almost disappeared from the discourse of the west European far right (which often proclaims its sympathies for Israel). In the Netherlands, Geert Wilders made the struggle against 'Islamo-fascism' his stock in trade. Consulted by referendum on 28 November 2010, 57 per cent of Swiss voters pronounced themselves in favour of a ban on minarets. Up until now, only four mosques out of 150 in the Swiss federation possess minarets, and this limit will remain unbreachable. In both France and Italy, several voices have been raised to propose similar measures, showing that, far from being a mania of the xenophobic and populist right in Switzerland, the desire to stigmatize Islam concerns Europe as a whole. Shlomo Sand is right to emphasize that Islamophobia today forms the cement of Europe – whose 'Judeo-Christian' matrix is constantly recalled – just as anti-Semitism played a fundamental role in the nineteenth century in the construction process of nationalisms.[31] Edward Said already observed that 'the transference of a popular anti-Semitic animus from a Jewish to an Arab target was made smoothly, since the figure was essentially the same'.[32] In the same line, Ithak Laor remarks that the polemics around the Islamic veil and the stubbornness with which Muslims are called on to assimilate, to conform to Western norms, reveal a significant forgetting of the ideological campaigns in which, between the Enlightenment and the Second World War, Jews were invited to abandon their difference, to 'improve' and 'civilize' themselves.[33]

As distinct from Judeophobia and anti-Semitism, now permanently stigmatized and repressed, Islamophobia is fully respectable, in a European culture whose colonial inheritance remains alive and well. Any manifestation of anti-Semitism arouses indignation and scandal, widely echoed in the media, whereas the discrimination daily affecting young people of African or Maghrebian origin who seek work, housing or simply access to a discotheque is part of everyday life. A name like Mohamed today brings inconveniences comparable with those experienced a century ago by Jews from eastern Europe who emigrated to Berlin, Vienna or Paris. An anti-Semitic handbook such as Édouard Drumont's *La France juive* would certainly not be tolerated today, and rightly so, but an essay like Oriana Fallaci's *The Rage and the Pride*, which is in many respects an Islamophobic equivalent, is an international bestseller.[34] Alain Finkielkraut, a leading representative of neoconservatism in France, recognizes a kernel of truth in the Italian journalist's pamphlet, admitting that he was 'struck, even captivated, by the sweep of her style and the force of her thought', despite regretting her outrageous comments that 'the sons of Allah breed like rats'.[35] Author 30 years ago of a brilliant essay on Jewish identity (*Le juif imaginaire*), the philosopher Finkielkraut is today engaged in a bitter battle against 'anti-white racism', left anti-racism, the multiculturalism of French society and Islamic obscurantism. Starting from these premises, he ends up with a pell-mell list of anti-Zionists, anti-racists and anti-fascists as his enemies:

> The future of hatred is in their camp and not of those faithful to Vichy. In the camp of the smile and not that of the grimace. Among humans and not among barbarians. In the camp of a mixed-race *society* and not that of an ethnic *nation*. In the camp of respect and not that of rejection… In the ranks of the unconditional champions of the Other and not of the blinkered petty-bourgeois who only love the Same.[36]

This high-flown prose attests to the relative legitimation that the far right enjoys from neoconservative ideology, because they share the same enemy: the immigrant, by preference Muslim. The immigrant today is a metaphorical figure, just as the Jew was for classical anti-Semitic discourse. When examined closely, the concept of xenophobia is not the most appropriate to characterize contemporary Islamophobia. What the European racists attack today in France is not the German or American foreigner, no more than in Germany it is the French or British. They attack the Maghrebian and the African, no matter whether they are immigrants or have been citizens of European Union countries for generations. Being unassimilable, the latter seem still more dangerous, as they corrupt the nation from within, altering its customs, distorting its language and lowering its culture.

Aggiornamento

The metamorphoses of racism, xenophobia and anti-Semitism cannot remain without political consequences. If the struggle against fascism is clearly a present issue in the new member states of the European Union, where we see today the rise of a nationalist, anti-Semitic and *fascisant* far right, the situation in the West is very different. Certainly, in a continent that has known Mussolini, Hitler and Franco, anti-fascism must remain part of democracy's cultural baggage, as a constitutive element of our historical consciousness. To struggle against the new forms of racism and xenophobia in the name of anti-fascism, however, risks falling into a rearguard battle, as we are not today defending a threatened democracy. Racism presents two complementary faces: on the one hand, that of the new 'republican' far right parties and groups, protectors of 'rights' defined on a ethnic, national or religious basis; on the other hand, that of government policies (detention camps for refugees, planned expulsions, laws that stigmatize and discriminate against ethnic or religious minorities). This new racism is quite compatible with representative democracy, reshaping this from within. It is thus democracy itself that must be reconsidered, along with notions of equality of rights and citizenship.

Just like anti-fascism, now ill-adapted to combat the new far right, the struggle against contemporary forms of Judeophobia is fuelled above all by the memory of the Shoah, an exterminatory anti-Semitism that corresponds neither to the reality nor to the ideologies and practices of anti-Jewishness in the twenty-first century. The mechanical transposition of past historical experiences onto the present is not always fruitful. It is subject both to anachronism and misunderstanding, dressing up its enemies in clothes that do not belong to them, and attributing to them intentions that are not theirs and belong to another epoch.

Instead of pursuing the phantoms of a past that is well inscribed in our memory, it would be more productive to confront the problems of the present, for which a good starting-point is Michel Wieviorka's lucid observation: without disappearing, anti-Semitism is in the process of being transformed into 'a secondary phenomenon, lacking both scope and any great capacity for mobilization, and combatted, each time it finds expression, in a way that is on the whole energetic and effective. It would be good if this could be the case for other forms of racism.'[37] If the end of Jewish modernity has one aspect about which we should incontestably rejoice, it is certainly this.

6
Zionism: Return to the Ethnos

After the Holocaust, as we saw in the first chapter, the birth of the state of Israel was a major moment in the reconfiguring of the 'Jewish question'. Not only because Israel shifted the very axis of Jewish existence – now redefined in relation to the genocide suffered and to a new state that claimed to represent Jewish existence – but also because it radically changed the image and perception of Jews in the world. A new actor had arisen alongside the diaspora, to give Jewishness a state dimension. If the whole of Jewish modernity had been focused on emancipation – acceptance and political recognition in the world of the gentiles – the proclamation of the Jewish state changed the basic situation. Some people saw this as the culmination of emancipation, others as a de-naturing of the diaspora vocation. The end of Jewish modernity blends here with another metamorphosis, whose ineluctable character Hannah Arendt grasped very well: the creation of a Jewish state, presented as the only way of acceding to full rights, corresponded with the birth of a new pariah people, the Palestinians, deprived of political recognition and rights. Jewish modernity arose with the challenge to an ancient oppression: it was incompatible with the transformation of oppressed into oppressors.

Historical contingency

Ever since its foundation Israel has been the object of conflicting teleological interpretations. For Zionists, it embodies the redemption of a people martyred by centuries of anti-Semitism, realizing a destiny inscribed in its history since the destruction of the Temple and the beginning of the diaspora (*galut*) in the first century CE; for defenders of the Palestinian cause, it forms the epilogue to a long history of Western imperialism and colonialism. Each of these readings, however, paints a black and white picture, one-sided and reductive. Far from being an age-old aspiration, the return to the 'land of our fathers' took shape only in the late nineteenth century, under the impulse of Theodor Herzl, with a nationalist movement that remained a small minority in the Jewish community until the Second World War. Its forerunners, from Moses Hess to Nathan Birnbaum and Leo Pinsker, had confined themselves to literary essays and the formation of small circles; and it was only a generation after the Zionist pioneers, in the interwar period, that Jewish immigration from eastern Europe gave the movement a truly colonizing character, well beyond the embryonic and almost philanthropic stage summed up by the classic definition: 'An American Jew gives money to a French Jew so that a Polish Jew can go and settle in Palestine.'[1] (A formula to which we should add the diplomatic role of the British Jewish patriarchate and the ideological framework provided by German-Jewish intellectuals.)

It would be hard to challenge the fact that Herzl belonged to the Orientalist and colonialist European culture of the nineteenth century. But as distinct from classic colonialism, Zionism did not want to seize a territory in order to plunder its resources and dominate its population, exploiting this as cheap labour-power; it aimed rather to establish a new society in the place of the indigenous one. Born as a movement of national liberation, it did not act in the name of imperialism, but it could not achieve its objectives without its support. Its leaders from Herzl onward were perfectly aware of this, and decided to combine the colonization of Palestine with intensive diplomatic activity. In other words, from the first Jewish settlements (the *yishuv*) of the late nineteenth century, through the Balfour declaration of 1917 to the foundation of Israel in 1948, the history of Zionism was that of a nationalism and colonialism *sui generis*. It would be equally hard to challenge, beyond the Zionist rhetoric, the vitality of the Israeli nation today, despite this having literally been 'invented' from every point of view: territorial, ethnic, political, cultural and even linguistic, thanks to the metamorphosis into a modern national language of an ancient idiom that for centuries had been relegated to a religious function.[2] This reality, however, was the result neither of providential design nor of fiendish imperial causality. Each of these teleologies, the negative one as much as the positive, is simplistic and reductive.

According to the historian Dan Diner, the state of Israel is the product of historical contingency.[3] It was born between the end of the Second World War and the outbreak of the Cold War, thanks to an exceptional and transitory moment of convergence between the great powers, in a world shattered by the discovery of the Holocaust and confronted with the problem posed by the hundreds of thousands of 'displaced persons' who had escaped the Nazi genocide and were temporally parked in refugee camps, and for whom a home had to be found.[4] Before the war, only the Zionist leadership thought of transforming into a state the small Jewish colony in Palestine (rescued by the Allied armies in winter 1942, when they stopped the advance of Rommel's *Afrikakorps* at El-Alamein). The British were hostile to this project, and very few Jews envisaged moving to Tel Aviv or Jerusalem, as against the millions who had left Europe for America. A few years later, in the epoch of decolonization, the Soviets would champion the cause of Arab nationalism and the great powers could no longer redraw the political frontiers of the Middle East as they saw fit. In short, we can view Israel as either a miracle or a tragedy of history, depending on our point of view, but certainly not as its ineluctable result. The Zionist movement included the whole spectrum of European nationalism, from the Marxist left to the semi-fascist right, as well as the most disparate versions of colonialism (from the most pacific to the most bellicose); Arab nationalism, for its part, was not different from most nationalisms in the colonial world. All were faced with a new and largely unforeseen situation.

The 1948 war, which broke out with Ben-Gurion's proclamation of Israel but had been preceded by a violent conflict between Jews and Arabs in the last months of the British mandate, following the United Nations (UN) vote in favour of the partition of Palestine, was the reflection of this historical contingency. For the parties in conflict, the legitimacy of their struggle was unquestionable. The Jewish soldiers drew their passion from the desire to redeem a past of humiliation and anti-Semitism; their action took place physically in Palestine, but their state of mind and their moral universe remained in Europe. On the Arab side, the war was experienced as a struggle designed to turn the page on European colonialism. In the eyes of world opinion, however, the Arab cause was identified not with a movement of national liberation but rather with a group of neo-feudal oligarchies whose opposition to British domination had led them to compromise with the Axis forces in the Second World War. (And who, in the 1948 conflict, were defending their particular interests, such as King Abdullah of

Jordan, who would fall victim to a Palestinian attack in 1951.) The Jews aroused the sympathy of the European countries, guilty of having powerlessly witnessed, if not collaborated in, the extermination of Jews by Nazism.[5] This state of mind explains the British passivity during the conflict, after four years of Zionist attacks against the mandate authority, the most bloody of which was the destruction by the Irgun of the British headquarters at the King David Hotel in Jerusalem, in July 1946, causing 93 deaths. The United Kingdom abstained in the UN partition vote, and its troops stood by and observed the massacres and expulsions of the Palestinians. This desire for reparations was explicitly brought up by Andrei Gromyko, the Soviet minister of foreign affairs, in a resounding speech at the UN in May 1947: 'The fact that no West European country has been able to ensure the defence of the basic rights of the Jewish people or to protect them against the violence unleashed by the fascist executioners explains the aspiration of the Jews to establish their own state. It would be unjust to deny them this right.'[6] The following year, Ilya Ehrenburg echoed this in asserting that the act of birth of the state of Israel had been written not with ink but with blood.[7] In 1948, the Soviets provided the Zionist forces with a military support that proved decisive. The Israeli army, formed from the Haganah, the Irgun and the Stern group militia, received arms from Czechoslovakia, while the Arab forces had only rather old British weapons and often lacked spare parts.

Only a few observers in 1947 had drawn conclusions from the first two Palestinian intifadas (in 1929 and 1936), or expressed doubts about the Zionist project, clearly formulated by Herzl in 1897, of creating in the Middle East a European state, 'an advance post against Asia', with a view to defending 'civilization against barbarism'.[8] Arab nationalists were not listened to, any more than the more clear-headed minds in the Zionist movement. And yet Ahad Haam, a Zionist pioneer, had warned from the start of Jewish colonization against a mythical view of Palestine as 'a land without people for a people without land'. As he wrote in 1891:

> We are accustomed to believing abroad that Palestine is a land almost entirely deserted, an uncultivated desert, a fallow field, where anyone who wishes to buy land can settle and acquire what he wants. In reality it is not so: in this whole land, it is hard to find an unsown

field... We are accustomed abroad to believe that the Arabs are desert savages, a people like donkeys, incapable of seeing and understanding what is happening around them. This is a great mistake.[9]

No one took seriously into consideration the idea of a binational state championed by the 'cultural Zionists' of the Brit Shalom movement (Martin Buber, Ernst Simon, Arthur Ruppin, and the rector of the Jewish University of Jerusalem, Yehudah Magnes), who were favourable to a national home but not to a Jewish state entity. What led the Western elites to decide to make the Arabs pay the price of the crimes perpetrated against the Jews in Europe by Nazism was simply a colonial prejudice – the view of the non-European world as a space to be hierarchically subjugated and thus culturally and politically mouldable.

Retrospectively (or prospectively), binationalism appears the only rational option, but its limitations are also quite clear. Both in its classic version, that of cultural Zionism, and in the more recent version within the Palestinian diaspora (Edward Said), it has always been an elitist movement, championed by far-sighted but isolated figures, whereas Jewish and Palestinian nationalisms have always been mass movements, endowed with wide networks in civil society and powerful armed wings.

Furthermore, the foundation of Israel led to a split within this minority of 'anti-state' Zionist intellectuals. As we saw, Hannah Arendt and Gershom Scholem had shared until 1946 the perspective of a binational state in which Arabs and Jews would coexist. But in 1948, Sholem accepted the foundation of a Jewish state and adapted his cultural Zionism to the fatal constraints of political Zionism and its *raison d'état*. Arendt did not follow him on this road, and their positions became irreconcilable. In 1948, Arendt published a text that today appears highly premonitory. If the Jews should win the war, she wrote, they would have to pay for the lasting consequences of their success:

> The 'victorious' Jews would live surrounded by an entirely hostile Arab population, secluded inside ever-threatened borders, absorbed with physical self-defence to a degree that would submerge all other interests and activities. The growth of a Jewish culture would cease to be the concern of the whole people; social experiments would

have to be discarded as impractical luxuries; political thought would centre around military strategy; economic development would be determined exclusively by the needs of war. And all this would be the fate of a nation that – no matter how many immigrants it could still absorb and how far it extended its boundaries... would still remain a very small people greatly outnumbered by hostile neighbours.[10]

The war of 1948 – the first of six Arab-Israeli wars – has recently been the object of a major historiographic revision that has definitively challenged the old Zionist thesis of the 'voluntary flight' of Palestinians in the confrontation between a Jewish 'David' and an Arab 'Goliath'. The account of the Nakba (catastrophe) given by the refugees has been confirmed by documents preserved in Israeli archives. There remains a divergence of interpretation that we can reduce, by analogy with the historiography of Nazism, to two distinct schools, one 'functionalist' and the other 'intentionalist'.[11] The leading representative of the former, Benny Morris, views the expulsion of more than 700,000 Palestinians as 'the result of a cumulative process and a set of causes';[12] the champions of the second, such as Ilan Pappe, depict a planned and systematic ethnic cleansing. This is not merely a question of methodological differences. Morris is a radical nationalist who, after having lucidly considered the expulsion of the Palestinians as the logical epilogue of the Zionist colonization project, regrets today that this ethnic cleansing was not more complete, given that its sequels continue to trouble Israel.[13] Pappe, for his part, has chosen to place his research in the service of the Palestinian cause, becoming the bête noire of the Israeli academic establishment. After working for several years at the University of Haifa, he now teaches in England, at the University of Exeter. Though they do not attribute the same importance to it, both schools have brought to light the existence of a project of forced evacuation, the famous 'Dalet plan', and documented massacres of Palestinians. From Der Yassin, a village on the outskirts of Jerusalem, to Tantura on the coast near Haifa, the violence of April and May 1948 presented all the typical features of civil war: destruction of houses, summary execution of civilians, collective rape of women. The Israeli general staff, moreover, used the Hebrew word *tihur*, meaning 'cleaning' or 'purification', more than 40 years before the concept of 'ethnic cleansing' was coined at the time of the wars in the former Yugoslavia.[14]

Arab atrocities, essentially reactive in kind, such as at Mount Scopus and Kfar Etzion, were far more limited, if only on account of the extremely unfavourable balance of forces. Arno J. Mayer, in the wake of Morris, has described Arab resistance to the expulsions as a spontaneous revolt, essentially infra-political, unorganized and lacking military leadership, corresponding rather to the model of the 'primitive rebels' described by Eric Hobsbawm in a classic study.[15] According to the Palestinian historian Rachid Khalidi, on the other hand, the formation of a Palestinian national consciousness preceded the first Israeli-Arab war. In his view, it goes back to the late nineteenth century and the twilight of the Ottoman empire, thanks to the efforts of an urban intelligentsia that had created some wide-ranging cultural institutions and a large number of periodicals.[16] But this involved only a small intellectual elite who lacked a political project. In 1948, the Arab armies were defeated because of their lack of unity, both politically and strategically. The most powerful and best organized of their number, the Jordanian army, wanted not to destroy Israel but to annex the West Bank. It would only be in the 1960s that Palestinian nationalism acquired an independent project and organization, with the foundation of the Palestine Liberation Organization.

Blood and faith

One thing is certain: the conduct of the Israeli army during the conflict fitted into the Zionist design of a Jewish state without Arabs. How could the Palestinians approve a partition plan that gave to the Jews, one quarter of the population, 60 per cent of the land? The war, moreover, allowed the Zionists to occupy a far larger territory than that originally envisaged in the UN's partition plan. In 1947, the Jews held around 10 per cent of the territory of mandate Palestine; in 1949, after the conflict and following the expropriation laws, they controlled some 85 per cent of this. The 'law of return' opened the gates of the new state to Jews from the whole world, while closing them at the same time to all those who had been driven off their lands (despite the UN resolution that envisaged restitution to its legitimate owners). Israel thus arose, in Perry Anderson's words, as 'a republic of blood and faith', a democracy, in other words, defined on a religious and ethnic basis, open to all who professed the Mosaic religion and all children of a Jewish mother, whatever their place of birth, yet closed to everyone else.[17] The first to benefit from the new law were the escapees from the Shoah, who found shelter in this way and, for many of them, a new homeland. They were followed, in an irony of history, by a large number of Jews from the Arab world whom Zionism had always ignored. Living embodiments of Oriental 'backwardness', these were subjected to an intense campaign of 'de-Arabization' and cultural assimilation by the Ashkenazi elite.[18] As for the Palestinians, they formed a new diaspora and filled refugee camps in all the bordering countries. Traumatized and powerless, the Arab minority that remained within the borders of the new state acquired a second-class citizenship. They continue today to live on their land, which has now become a foreign country in which they are perceived as a kind of 'fifth column' of the Arab enemy.[19] While it offered citizenship to the survivors of the Nazi genocide – a third of the Israeli population in the 1950s – the new state thus created a mass of Palestinian refugees, real pariahs in Hannah Arendt's sense of the term: human beings without a state, deprived of the 'right to have rights'. Today, as we shall go on to see, the memory of these victims is fundamentally incompatible with that of the Holocaust of which Israel sees itself as guardian and redeemer. The Hebrew state cannot accept that it was born out of a war that may indeed have been experienced as a struggle for national liberation, but that acquired, both in its conception and its application, the features of a generalized ethnic cleansing.

The building of Israel in Palestine was thus effected at the price of a triple negation. First of all, a negation of the Jewish diaspora – paradoxical in this case, since Israel sought to put an end to the European diaspora by constructing a Western state in Palestine. The second and third negations, on the other hand, present a strong Orientalist dimension. Zionism wanted to wipe out Arab Palestine, by denying the existence of an Arab culture and nation that was in the process of formation: a mass of fellahin was not a national community. And finally, a negation of the Jewish diaspora in the Arab world. If the Jewish state had been built on the European model, then Oriental Jews had to assimilate Western culture in order to become full members of it. They were originally accepted as a kind of ersatz for their fellow religionists exterminated in Europe, to be 'regenerated' by their incorporation into a modern Western nation. Zionism never viewed Jews of Arab language and culture as a bridge between a society of European origin and its Arab environment. Their 'return to history' signified the negation of their own history and their incorporation in a Western history.[20]

There thus began, in a fortress endowed with increasingly powerful weapons and before long the atomic bomb, the construction of an 'imaginary community' under the sign of the Bible, ecology, the West, and, as we shall see, of the Shoah. In the final analysis, it is the Bible that legitimizes for Zionists the right of Jews to occupy Palestine. The ecology of verdant forests hides Palestinian villages that were destroyed and wiped off the map. The West, in the end, is the matrix of a state built by European colonists and today the strategic ally of the United States. Everyone brought their own contribution to this national construction: from the activists of the kibbutzim (often more military outposts than islands of social equality) to the architects who redesigned towns, to the philologists, historians and archaeologists who stubbornly worked to recover an age-old Jewish Palestine under the ruins of modern Arab Palestine. As Ilan Pappe has written, 'The archaeological zeal to reproduce the map of "Ancient" Israel was in essence none other than a systematic, scholarly, political and military attempt to deArabize the terrain – its names and geography, but above all its history.'[21] Behind this façade, however, the contradictions of a paradoxical success lie concealed. Zionism was born, according to its founders, in order to definitively remove Jews from the ghettos into which Christian Europe had enclosed them and to which modern anti-Semitism tried to return them. Israel today plans to construct the walls of a new ghetto – both metaphorical and material – in which to enclose the Jews in order to protect them, by separating them hermetically from the world around them.

According to the historian David Biale, Zionism, despite its promises to the contrary, was bound to maintain a certain continuity with the many centuries of Jewish life in the diaspora.[22] The new state existence of Jews in Israel did not modify their submission to an external authority in relation to which their power is defined (not without tensions and conflicts, as shown by the relationship between Obama and Netanyahu). In today's globalized world, the old model of the royal alliance seems reborn in the form of a Jewish state protected by the planet's dominant political and military power, for which it is a piece in its mechanism of hegemony. Born from a desperate will to survive, and strengthened by exploiting contradictions between the great powers, Israel has finally settled into a relationship of alliance with and submission to the United States, where its cause can find ardent defenders, both in the state apparatus and the wider society. Conditions have changed, but this expansionist, powerful and warlike state still remains dependent on an external support. Its sovereignty, in the last analysis, remains limited.

Israel and the Shoah

The Shoah and Israel are indissociable. Not simply because the Jewish state was born in 1948 thanks to an agreement between the great powers, and to a UN vote aiming to 'compensate' Jews for the Nazi genocide; not only, therefore, because the Shoah constitutes its historical premise and background, but also and above all because it constitutes a pillar of its national consciousness. Israel is the heir to the Shoah, if only because it received several hundred thousand survivors from the great Nazi massacre. Over the years, it has redefined its identity by seeking to become the representative and ultimately the redeemer of the Holocaust victims. The tragic event that permitted its birth has gradually become its main historical justification and, once inscribed in its national messianism, the pretext constantly invoked to legitimize its actions. In other words, the memory of the Holocaust was grafted onto the trunk of Zionism to become the matrix of a political religion: Israeli nationalism. This provided the cement for the construction of a Jewish nation formed out of disparate groups, coming not only from Europe but also from North Africa and the Middle East, and surrounded by a hostile Arab world. We should not confuse this memory with the individual testimonies of the escapees from the death camps, even if it superimposes itself on these and feeds off them. It is a matter of representation, a national narrative elaborated within Israeli society and fostered by its governments, whether labour or right-wing. This memory thus completes the foundations of the Israeli 'imaginary community', allowing it to transcend the briefness of its existence and the heterogeneity of its own composition.[23]

The incorporation of this past within Israeli memory, however, was not immediate. In the 1950s, when the trauma of genocide remained very acute and the death camp survivors made up a considerable proportion of Israeli society, the Shoah was absent from official discourse. A silent and discrete work of mourning coexisted with public repression. Reasserting a Zionist stereotype, Ben-Gurion would declare that Jewish history was interrupted in 135 BC, when the Romans repressed the Bar Kochba revolt, and only continued its path with the foundation of Israel. As a people without a state, the Jews thus became, in Hegelian terms, a 'people without history'. The Zionist palingenesis restored to them a national dignity lost for centuries. The rise of Israel was thus intended as a radical rupture with the diaspora, the place of humiliation, persecution and degradation, and presented itself as the necessary alternative to 'exile', the *galut*, considered a real malady. Far from being persecuted, the Israeli 'new Jew' was a colonist, a farmer and a fighter. The new state did not want to appear as the receptacle of a people of victims, or to identify with the skeletal figures of the Auschwitz survivors. In the nationalist clichés of the time, its sons should be proud, sporting and muscular. A tradition thus had to be 'invented', one that, while preserving certain striking moments of Jewish history, could extract these from the diaspora and annex them to a national epic embodied by Zionism. The image of deported Jews did not suit the *völkisch* canons of Zionism, too closely recalling the idea that its ideologists, in particular Max Nordau, presented Jewish 'degeneration' as a fatal mixture of weakness, impotence, passivity, lack of character and spirit of submission.[24] If we compare the portrait of the Jew drawn by anti-Semitism in literature with the iconography of the diaspora Jew cultivated by Zionism, the difference is rather slight.

The 'new Jew' was a *Muskeljude*, respectful of racial codes and the genre of nationalism, rather than a victim. This was how the refugees on the *Exodus* – a ship loaded with survivors from the Nazi camps who spent months in 1947 travelling back and forth on the sea before landing in Palestine after overcoming the British obstacles to their disembarkation – were transformed into fighters and heroes who, at the price of countless sacrifices, paved the way to national renaissance.[25] It was also how the Warsaw ghetto uprising, in spring 1943, was revisited as a patriotic action and a 'Zionist gesture'. And again, how the account of the insurrection written by Marek Edelman, one of its leaders – at the time an activist in the Bund, the anti-Zionist Jewish socialist party, who chose after the war to remain in Poland – was only translated into Hebrew very belatedly by a small publisher. 'The flourishing industry of memory that had to develop in Israel around the Jewish rebellion and its heroes,' writes Idith Zertal, 'had no place for Edelman and his version of the facts.'[26] Still today, the postulate that contrasts the authenticity of Israeli national existence with the inauthenticity of diaspora life remains a rubric of the Zionist intelligentsia, conjugated in different modes. The writer Avraham B. Yeoshua persists in defining the diaspora as 'exile', seeing in it the marks of a 'neurotic solution' to which he opposes Zionism as 'Jewish normality'.[27] The historian David Vital, author of a monumental history of the European Jews from the French Revolution to the Second World War, estimates for his part that 'the diaspora dishonoured Jews'.[28]

The decisive turn, the moment at which Israel ceased to view the Shoah as the paroxysmic manifestation of a shameful past and began to explicitly claim its memory as a legitimizing source of its politics, was the Eichmann trial in 1961. Ben-Gurion sought to make a 'sacred experience' out of it, an admonition addressed to the whole world and a pedagogic act for the Israeli population. In his eyes, this trial largely transcended the individual responsibilities of one of the architects of the 'final solution'. He defined it as 'the trial of the Jewish people against the eternal anti-Semitism in all countries and all generations'.[29]

It was the Eichmann trial, as we saw, that completed the break between Arendt and Scholem, the former reproaching the latter for having fallen into a view of Jewish history that equated this with a kind of mystic entity – perhaps because he identified mimetically with the object of his studies.[30] In this historical conjuncture, Arendt's *Selbstdenken* came into conflict with the Jewish perception of the Shoah for which Scholem became a spokesman. Arendt had taken the measure of the event already during the war – in a well-known interview, she would say how she felt an abyss opening under her feet. The Eichmann trial, on the other hand, was when the world became properly acquainted with the Nazi genocide. This was the first time, giving evidence at this trial, that survivors from the Nazi camps were able to express themselves before the whole world with the sense of being heard. Arendt, in her essay, deepened a reflection she had begun 20 years earlier, but she did not take precautions in addressing herself to an international opinion that had only just come to realize what the Holocaust had been, to a Jewish diaspora that had repressed it, and to a state of Israel that now found itself confronting the trauma from which it had been born. The timescale for elaboration of critical thought does not always coincide with the construction time of collective memory. There can be a discordance, as the Eichmann trial proved. Arendt was unaware of this, or decided to ignore it.

After having proved its capacity to render justice in the name of the Jewish people, Israel no longer had any need to conceal the Shoah. On the contrary, it could mobilize the memory of this to transform its policies into an action of reparation. It became commonplace, for Israeli ministers and officials, to assimilate Arab rejection to the secular history of European anti-Semitism, and compare Arab and Muslim leaders to Hitler – from Nasser to Arafat, Saddam Hussein to Ahmadinejad. Many intellectuals have lent themselves to this 'Nazification' of the enemy. The writer and Noble laureate Elie Wiesel celebrated the Israeli victory in the Six Day War of 1967 with a nationalist pathos worthy of the early Ernst Jünger: 'Two thousand years of suffering, waiting and hope have been mobilized in this battle, as well as the millions of victims of the Shoah. Like clouds of fire, they have come to the help of their heirs. And no enemy will ever be capable to conquer them.'[31] The victims of the Shoah became a posteriori martyrs in the Zionist cause. The victory was sacralized and the occupation of the Palestinian territories confirmed as a necessary guarantee against the threat represented by the ineluctable hostility of the surrounding world.

Political theology

Taking up a classic formula of Carl Schmitt, Dan Diner defines Israel as 'a theologico-political project of modernity'.[32] Zionism, appropriating the ideology and language of twentieth-century nationalisms, secularized a millennial history whose postulate lay in the identity between a people and a religion. It gave birth to a *sui generis* form of nationalism, not a traditional nation-state but a nation in permanent construction. A particular relationship between Zionism and religion followed from this. Is it in the strict sense a political religion? This concept defines a secular and even atheist ideology that replaces traditional religions and imposes itself by the sacralization of its own values, by the adhesion of its followers on the basis of a belief and by its mobilization in ritualized forms. The political Zionism of its founders – from Herzl to Borochov, Ahad Haam to Jabotinsky – contained all the features of a secular religion. Once in power, however, it was caught up in its own contradictions. It did not substitute itself for religion but instead reinterpreted this. It sought to be, and still does seek to be, the modern way of realizing the age-old prayers and aspirations of generations of Jews. In other words, Zionism neither abandoned nor replaced religion, it simply gave it a national dimension. Israel's national symbols have their meaning in this context: the seven-branched candelabra (menorah) and the flag. The menorah symbolizes the Hebrew temple; the flag takes the colours of the prayer shawl. Despite asserting its secular character, the state thus gives itself a theologico-political mission. Israeli secularity does not refer to an ideal of citizenship defined on the basis of non-denominational criteria. In the words of Raz-Krakotzkin, 'the opposition between secular and religious masks the theological and colonial aspects that the Israeli definition of secularism contains'. This latter, he explains, 'relates to a colonial theological consciousness that views itself as depository of a final and definitive interpretation of the holy scriptures'.[33] Zeev Sternhell reaches a similar conclusion when, after describing Zionism as 'a response typical of Herder, if not indeed tribal, to the challenge of emancipation' and the crisis of European liberalism, he goes on to recall the 'supreme argument' of this ethnic nationalism: the Bible.[34] And David Biale points out the irony of a secular movement that has built a state obliged to have recourse to religion in order to promulgate its laws, to define access to citizenship, legitimize its frontiers and orient its foreign policy.[35] From the 1960s on, this eschatological vision of Israel as the providential destiny of the people of the Book was combined with a new identity centred on the Shoah, which saw in Jewish suffering the legitimacy of a redeeming state. Even as a political religion, therefore, Zionism is a phenomenon *sui generis*. It effects a fusion between the secularization of an old messianism (the return to Eretz Israel) and the sacralization of the memory of a profane historical experience (the extermination of six million Jews).

The conflict with the Arab world becomes only the more acute when, after the defeat of all secular perspectives – from pan-Arabism to socialism, not to mention the discrediting of liberal democracy, identified with the West's imperial policy – the Palestinians seek an issue in religious nationalism in the form of Islamism.

Israel finds itself today facing a dilemma. In the longer term, there is only one alternative. It can embark on the path of binationalism, dismantling its colonies surrounded by barbed wire and constructing with the Palestinians a political community that belongs to all its citizens, without ethnic, linguistic, cultural or religious discrimination, without a 'right of return' reserved for Jews throughout the world but denied to the Palestinians who were expelled from their land. Or it can remain a 'Jewish state', with a democracy that will inevitably come to increasingly resemble the ancient *millet* system of the Ottoman empire: no longer an Islamist state committed to protecting its Christian and Jewish citizens, but a Jewish state that finds ever more awkward the presence within its frontiers of a growing Muslim minority.[36] Its fate will then fatally follow that of South Africa under apartheid, and in the long run, neither the Bible nor the atom bomb will manage to save it.[37]

The Zionism of its founders sought to emancipate Jews in the context of a modern nation-state. Like any nationalism, its ideology drew on an ancestral mythology but was projected towards the future: the Jewish nation had a long history, but once it gave itself a state existence, it would fit into modernity. The upheavals of the twentieth century enabled it to carry out its project but, by a kind of historical irony, Israel put an end to Jewish modernity. Diaspora Judaism had been the critical conscience of the Western world; Israel survives as one of its mechanisms of domination.

7
Memory: The Civil Religion of the Holocaust

The last chapter of this book studied the memory of the Shoah. Jewish modernity was accompanied throughout its trajectory by the shadow of anti-Semitism, a prejudice sometimes subterranean and subtle, sometimes expressed in overt and violent forms. The end of this modernity, therefore, was expressed not only in the decline of anti-Semitism, as analysed in Chapter 5, but also by the transformation of the memory of the Holocaust into a kind of 'civil religion' of the Western world, a necessary standard for measuring the moral virtues of its democracies and the test to which those states that wish to integrate into its political institutions are subjected.

Secular religions

The first formulation of the concept of 'civil religion' goes back to Rousseau. In a famous passage of his *Social Contract* (book 4), he describes this as a 'purely civil profession of faith' that aims to arouse among human beings a 'sentiment of sociability'. As a champion of separation between church and state, Rousseau held that the latter should respect the religious beliefs of its citizens, and stood for the principle of an ethos shared by its members so that they would love their duties. 'The dogmas of civil religion must be simple', he continued, indicating, besides a vague deism, general norms such as 'the happiness of the just, the punishment of evil-doers, the sanctity of the social contract', as well as the rejection of intolerance. Nearly a century and a half later, under the Third Republic, Émile Durkheim referred to the tendency, typical of the French Revolution, to transforms 'things purely secular in nature' such as homeland, liberty and reason into 'sacred things', thus establishing a new secular religion 'with its dogma, symbols, altars, and holidays'.[1] Patriotism was one of the features of this secular religion, which Durkheim himself saw as a natural duty.

The civil religions arose from secularization, the process through which in the modern age the religious gave way to the profane, both in representations of the world and in political institutions. But the retreat of religion, steadily supplanted by reason and science in the explanation of reality, was not necessarily accompanied by the decline of the sacred. Secularization was rather manifested in the form of a *transfer of sacrality* towards symbols, objects and institutions belonging to the profane world, which were thus charged with an aura that only gods, prophets and saints could previously claim.[2] This gave rise to what Raymond Aron called 'secular religions', in other words, 'doctrines that in the souls of our contemporaries take the place of a vanished faith and situate the salvation of humanity here on earth, in the distant future in the form of a social order to be created'.[3] These lines, written in 1944, refer in particular to the ideologies of the first half of the twentieth century, communism and the various forms of fascism, which other writers had already described as 'political religions'.[4]

Beyond the particular context in which it was elaborated, the concept of secular religion illuminates several aspects of modernity. Alongside the totalitarian ideologies that imposed themselves as a substitute for religion and sought to achieve salvation by the action of a movement, a party or a regime, often identified with a charismatic leader invested with a quasi-divine office, there have been civil religions respectful of democracy and liberties.[5] Far from being opposed to pluralism and the rule of law, the sacralization of politics that these civil religions proclaimed had the effect of instituting a shared ethos in the Rousseauian sense. After the model of the French Revolution which, by its secular festivals and especially the proclamation under the Convention of the 'cult of the supreme being', launched a vast campaign to promote republican values (justice, liberty, equality, humanity, the people, etc.),[6] all modern democracies have proceeded to the sacralization of their institutions. This does not mean that they substituted faith for rational adhesion (made possible by pluralism and tested in elections), rather that they aroused a belief and an emotional attachment – Durkheim called it a 'mystical effervescence' – to the myths, symbols and institutions of the state. The flag, monuments, anniversaries, celebrations, festivals and commemorations are the emblems and rituals by which modern states have attempted, as civil religions, to take root and legitimize themselves with peoples. Creating a mystique of the flag, commemorating the dead and making sanctuaries of places of memory, along with compulsory schooling and military service, are ways in which nations have built themselves as 'imagined communities'.[7]

Up till now, civil religions have essentially taken national forms, as shown by French republicanism, whose foundations were laid down by the Revolution but which was given definitive shape by the Third Republic, and American patriotism, founded on the myth of a great nation blessed by God, charged with implementing a providential grand design of freedom and democracy (defended and, if necessary, exported through force).[8] The democracies of the twentieth century have also known supranational civil religions, such as the pacifism that followed the Great War, or antifascism in the 1930s and 1940s, particularly in the time of the Spanish civil war and the Resistance, but their influence was fragmentary and discontinuous. Pacifism was only an ephemeral flame, soon replaced by the call to arms against Nazism and the Axis powers. It experienced a revival after 1945, under the impact of Hiroshima and Nagasaki, but never managed to overcome the cleavages of the Cold War. Antifascism began its decline at the same time, on account of its gradually increasing identification with communism when it became a state ideology in the Soviet bloc countries. Even in Italy, a country where it was a unifying experience of the 'first republic', it ceased to be a consensual and shared reference.

A global civil religion

At this time in the twenty-first century, it is the memory of the Holocaust that fills the role of a global civil religion.[9] It sacralizes certain values inherited from the Enlightenment – human rights, pluralism, tolerance, respect for the other, rejection of racism and anti-Semitism – that form the moral foundation of liberal democracy. Like any secular religion, it is a combination of dogmas, beliefs and symbols that are proclaimed and spread by ritualized practices. It fashions the legacy of the Holocaust into a kind of precept of universal scope, embodied and protected by a number of supranational institutions. Quite clearly, this civil religion is linked to the testimonies of the survivors of the death camps, who for a long time remained hidden and discreet, and to the critical reflection aroused by the crimes of Nazism, from which it sought to draw universal lessons. It is a response to the need to 'moralize history' that Jean Améry felt in his solitary and bitter meditations on his experience of the concentration camp,[10] but it transforms this demand into a moral injunction. Solemn and official, bearing the seal of great institutions (states, European Union, United Nations Educational, Cultural and Scientific Organization (UNESCO), etc.), it embalms history. It is rather similar, in this respect, to the monuments to the dead of the Great War that froze the memory of another holocaust (the word is appropriate in this case, as soldiers were called on to sacrifice their lives for their homeland), or to the monuments of actually existing socialism that immortalized – and neutralized – the memory of the October revolution. Clearly, to call this memorialization 'global' does not mean that it has the same significance or the same forms in Germany, the United States or China. But there can be no doubt that it lies at the root of a new attention for victims across the planet, and offers a model of reference for all demands for recognition, justice and reparations (symbolic, material, memorial) bound up with the suffering generated by the violence of the twentieth century. The memory of colonial genocides and massacres would not be the same without the institutionalization of the memory of the Holocaust in Europe. The irruption of memory into the diplomatic relations of China and South Korea with Japan fits into this context.

The civil religion of the Holocaust has its particular doctrine: the uniqueness of the event, which some people try to distinguish terminologically from other genocides and make into a myth, postulating its metaphysical and transcendent character, and denouncing any reduction as abusive.[11] They defend this idea as a dogma that requires no explanation but must be believed as an article of faith. The Shoah, as an unrepresentable and inconceivable event, is then transformed into an object of cult and commemoration, capable of arousing intense emotions but removed from any critical understanding and analysis: 'Here there is no "why"' (*Hier ist kein Warum*), Claude Lanzmann concluded, echoing an SS saying related by Primo Levi.[12] Dogmas and faith require places of ritual, a demand met by the memorials that exist in many cities – the oldest being Vad Vashem, created in Jerusalem in 1953, followed by the memorial of the unknown Jewish martyr in Paris inaugurated three years later, and more recently the enormous Holocaust-Mahnmal in Berlin, inaugurated in 2005 – and the extermination sites, today preserved as museums and joined by other museums such as those in Washington, Paris and Mexico. This civil religion possesses its icons (well-known victims such as Anne Frank) and its 'secular saints' (those survivors who bore witness, such as Primo Levi, despite his own definition of survivors as secondary, 'not the true witnesses'),[13] not forgetting its 'secular priests', likewise against their grain (Imre Kertesz, Nobel laureate for literature) or completely immersed in their pastoral mission (Elie Wiesel, Nobel Peace Prize). The liturgy of this civil religion is deployed on the occasion of anniversaries, with public commemorations often mediatized or institutionalized, such as 'days of memory', and with visits by school groups to the extermination camps. In a secular world, the cultural industry – cinema in particular – serves as a fundamental vector of diffusion for the memory of the Shoah. Playing on two distinct registers, that of fiction and that of testimony, Steven Spielberg and Claude Lanzmann have been the major architects of this, their creations giving rise to a whole genre that has several followers, more or less talented.

The stages

This civil religion has undergone a very long process of incubation. Our perception of the Holocaust today is very different from that which prevailed in 1945, at the end of the Second World War. The pervasive presence of anti-Semitism in mentalities and culture contributed to indifference and incomprehension on the part of a section of public opinion, but the reasons for the silence of that time probably run deeper than this. As we saw in connection with the Eichmann trial, consciousness and thought do not always have an immediate grasp on events, sometimes requiring a longer time for development. The genocide of Europe's Jews was initially 'submerged' in the wider violence of the Second World War. At Nuremberg, in 1945, it was treated as one war crime among others. The culture of the time was dominated by antifascism, and more ready to value the legacy of political deportation than to meditate on a genocide perpetrated in the name of a project of racial domination. The symbol of Nazi barbarity was not Auschwitz but Buchenwald, where so many antifascists were murdered. This culture seemed then to link up with the tradition of the Enlightenment and the idea of progress. Once Nazism was eliminated, civilization could pursue its course. The Cold War marked the return of West Germany to the Atlantic camp, and the crimes of the Nazis were put in brackets, not to say forgotten. The requirements of the struggle against totalitarian communism authorized the forgetting of Nazi totalitarianism, and several leading figures of the Third Reich were recycled in the Adenauer governments. The same tendency could be seen right across Europe, in differing forms and degrees, the amnesty laws promulgated in practically every country serving as a reflection of this. In France, as François Azouvi has recently shown, the postwar years were marked by a debate on the singularity of the Jewish extermination, with Catholic voices making their mark as well as Jewish ones.[14] But this debate was not enough to prevent the repression of the crime in the public sphere. Even the survivors of the death camps did not want to singularize their suffering, but rather integrate back into their national communities on a basis of equality. Time was needed before the Holocaust imposed itself at the centre of the Western world's historical consciousness.

On a global scale, the coming of the 'age of the witness', in Annette Wieviorka's striking expression,[15] dates from the Eichmann trial in Jerusalem in 1961. This was when international opinion discovered the Holocaust, and the survivors of the death camps felt they had finally been heard. A new perception asserted itself: Nazi extermination was no longer regarded as the expression of a retreat of civilization into barbarism, but rather as a barbarism inscribed in modernity itself, which showed its destructive side to the light of day. In the immediate postwar period, witnesses were ignored, just as critics of progress were viewed as followers of an incurable form of romanticism. Primo Levi's *If This is a Man* was initially published in a small print run by an obscure publisher. An understanding of the devastating effects of instrumental reason coincided with the emergence of the figure of the death camp survivor as privileged witness of his or her century. This shift was profound. There were also other moments in the collective anamnesis that placed Nazi crimes at the centre of Western culture, from the broadcasting of the TV series *Holocaust* to the *Historikerstreit* in Germany and the French debate on Holocaust denial or 'negationism'.

Today, the twentieth century has come to be seen as the century of Auschwitz: the genocide of the Jews has given way to an omnipresent memory in the public sphere. The transition from repression to obsessive memorialization implies a significant shift in representations of the past. During the phase of forgetting, the dominant idea was that of 'mastering the past', *Vergangenheitsbewältigung*, which Levi saw as a pure and simple 'imposture' consisting of 'forgetting everything and forgiving everything'.[16] The silence about the past was then justified in the name of 'superseding' it and achieving reconciliation. The stage of anamnesis and obsessive memorialization, on the other hand, is when the idea of a 'past that will not pass' is dominant. Faced with a wall of silence and indifference, witnesses used to oppose their memory to a forgetful society. Primo Levi spoke of testimony as both therapeutic and pedagogic: therapeutic for the victims deprived of recognition, and pedagogic for a society guilty of forgetting and indifference.[17] When Adorno offered his slogan, 'Never again Auschwitz' in 1966, as a kind of new categorical imperative bequeathed by the Nazi era,[18] there was nothing commonplace about his stand; it appeared rather as a very salutary provocation. Today, the 'duty of memory' has become a rhetorical discourse, rather conformist, and used as a ritual formula.

Certainly the civil religion of the Holocaust possesses its virtues. It reveals a new sensitivity towards human rights, and expresses a shared historical consciousness of Europe's criminal past. In Germany, the memory of Nazi crimes has become a real pillar of national identity, as attested by the Holocaust memorial erected in Berlin close to the Reichstag. Just as in the nineteenth century anti-Semitism was a cultural code making possible a negative definition of German national identity, so today this function is fulfilled by the Holocaust. After Auschwitz, Jürgen Habermas wrote, nationalism has no more validity; the only patriotism admissible is *Verfassungspatriotismus* (patriotism to the constitution).[19] In the first years of the new century, Germany has even rewritten its nationality code, ceasing to conceive itself as an ethnic nation in favour of becoming a community of citizens. In international football games, Germans identify with a team whose stars bear Polish, Turkish, Spanish and Ghanaian names. The memory of the Holocaust plays its part in this metamorphosis.

The final stage in this long process of constructing a global civil religion consists in making it the paradigm for a reactivation of the past that equally affects other communities, other historical experiences, other victims and other memories. This is the inevitable and logical consequence of its universal vocation (despite the rhetoric of uniqueness). The anamnesis extends to other genocides forgotten or deprived of recognition (such as those of the Hereros of south-west Africa and of the Armenians), to other political victims (those of the Latin American military dictatorships, those of Soviet communism), even touching more distant times (slavery, colonialism, the conquest of the New World). But this view of the past focused almost exclusively on its victims is not without danger; it risks becoming a distorting prism that impoverishes history. With the victims now recognized as the true heroes of the past, the agents of history have to transform themselves into victims in order to take their place in collective representations. This tendency leads to a mutilated historical hermeneutic, suppressing the plurality of historical subjects. If a Jewish child gassed at Auschwitz is incontestably an innocent victim, the Warsaw ghetto insurgents were also fighters, who precisely chose to escape the role of victim that their persecutors assigned them. They died arms in hand, and to view them merely as victims does not do them justice. The militants from the Chilean Movimiento de Izquierda Revolucionaria (MIR) or Argentinian Ejército Revolucionario del Pueblo (ERP) who fell under the repression of the Latin American dictatorships were certainly killed by regimes that trampled over human rights, but they saw themselves as combatants in a civil war, and it was on account of their political actions that they were persecuted. It is customary today, in both of these countries, to use the term 'genocide' for the bloody repression conducted by the military dictatorships of the 1970s. This enables these countries to meet the commemorative norms of the globalized world, but it hardly helps an understanding of the past. After having closed a long period of repression and amnesia, the age of the witness now risks leading to a black-and-white view of history. Pity for the dead obscures the picture, and stands in the way of a historical consciousness that pays attention to the complexity of the past.

Lachrymose history

The civil religion of the Holocaust exhumes an ancient view of Jewish history as the tragic epic of a community united and perpetuated by pain. This representation reappears today to define a minority whose cement is no longer religion. The mirror of this 'lachrymose history' is the suffering gaze of Elie Wiesel, Nobel laureate, that Christ-like sums up Jewish pain and the desire for the West to expiate its age-old past of anti-Semitism.[20] As Esther Benbassa has shown, this is not a new vision.[21] It goes back to the Renaissance, when Jospeh Ha-Cohen, a Jew expelled from Spain after the Reconquista, published in Italy a book titled *The Valley of Tears* (1558); it was reformulated in the nineteenth century by the first Jewish historians. In the 1850s, Heinrich Graetz published a monumental *Geschichte der Juden*, conceiving this as a long martyrology brought to an end by emancipation.[22] This lachrymose vision reappeared after the Second World War with a different end in view. On the one hand, it reinforced an interpretation of the history of anti-Semitism as a linear movement, from the persecutions of the Christian Middle Ages to the Nazi gas chambers. Jewish history thus became an interminable way of the cross, the extermination camps being only its logical and coherent culmination. On the other hand, it contributed to the construction of a public memory of the Nazi genocide. Thus, there arose a theology of the Shoah as a unique event, the summit of a long road of suffering, a sacred event and thus distinct from any other historical violence. In parallel with this, a kind of secular theodicy equally developed, making Israel, the state born as a response to the genocide, an equally sacred entity. It was the Canadian theologian Emil Fackenheim in particular, drawing on the Kabbalist theory of *tikkun*, reparation for an 'original cosmogonic damage', who presented Israel as a redemptive act for Jewish suffering, as sacred as the tragic event that gave rise to it.[23] The Holocaust thus confers on Israel the status of representative of the victims, and legitimizes it as redemptive. The Tsahal is no longer an army of occupation but rather an organ of self-defence for a threatened people. 'Our army is pure', the Israeli generals maintain in *Tsahal*, a film conceived by Claude Lanzmann as the epilogue to his *Shoah*. In the Christian world, this view corresponds to a representation of Jewish history as a martyrology culminating in the figure of the 'crucified Jew'. Marc Chagall illustrated this by painting a famous series of Christian allegories, and in 1979 Pope Jean-Paul II defined Auschwitz as a 'Golgotha of the contemporary world'.[24]

The Holocaust and law

The civil religion of the Holocaust grants the state new prerogatives. The proclamation of days of memory, the erection of monuments, the establishment of museums and memorial sites, all presuppose legislative intervention. In other words, memory is institutionalized; it becomes official discourse, alongside and sometimes in competition with a history – the writing of history – that seeks to be a critical discourse about the past. Its legal enactment creates a new dialectic between history and law. Law transforms memory into a 'mechanism',[25] an instrument for framing and formatting the past.

The constitutive tie that links history to law should not be underestimated, but since antiquity history has freed itself from law, and the new mixing of genres typical of our day is not without posing certain problems. It is undeniable that justice may intervene in the elaboration of collective memory, allowing a page to be turned, a break to be marked, pushing into the sphere of the past what had until now appeared as the present. The memory of the Second World War would not be the same without the Nuremberg trial, nor that of the Holocaust without the Eichmann trial. In all these cases, law responded to a demand for justice that arose in society. On the other hand, the records of trials often offer historians sources of utmost importance. Law, memory and history constitute three different modalities by which a society defines its relationship to the past. These three dimensions coexist and are often superimposed, but it is useful to bear in mind the differences that divide them. The institutionalization of memory, however, seems to muddy the traces.

National parliaments, concerned to apply the virtues of a memory erected into civil religion, have seen a legislative proliferation that frames the past in criminal as well as symbolic terms. On the one hand, they have voted laws that establish days of remembrance, museums and memorial sites.[26] On the other hand, they promulgate repressive laws that punish the denial of certain crimes, and make new prosecutions possible by abolishing the statute of limitations. New trials thus apply a belated political justice, sometimes several decades after the alleged facts, as we have seen with the Barbie and Papon trials in France, the Priebke trial in Italy, the trial of Demianiuk in Germany and so on.

As for the anti-negationist laws adopted in various European countries, including France and Germany, after several years in force these have largely proved their harmful character. First of all, they have had the perverse effect of transforming the 'assassins of memory' into 'victims'. Negationists try to legitimize their lies in the name of freedom of expression. Another perverse effect has been the extreme mediatization of all the trials, verdicts or arrests arising from the application of these laws, which have thus paradoxically become vehicles of propaganda. The arrest in Vienna of the British negationist David Irving focused the attention of the global media. His American counterpart Arthur Butz, however, can publish his pamphlets with total impunity, there being no laws against this, but also to total indifference, as no US newspapers or TV channels find him newsworthy.

The French law of 2006 that penalizes denial of the Armenian genocide shows that the legal repression of denial of the Shoah set a legal precedent. In a context that favours the emergence of victims, these laws can only multiply. To establish an exceptional regime for the Holocaust, or for a limited number of genocides, actually amounts to establishing a de facto hierarchy among the victims.[27] Establishing a special legislation for one particular group is not only morally unacceptable, it is also politically dangerous.

Apart from these pragmatic considerations, these laws are debatable for a deeper reason: they contribute to establishing an official norm in the interpretation of the past, transforming historical truth into state truth. This has aroused criticism from a large number of historians. In France, some of the most eminent of these launched an appeal, 'Freedom for history' in December 2005, calling for the abolition of several 'laws of memory'.[28] This appeal triggered a wide social debate around a basic principle of democracy: historical truth needs no legal protection, it should be the result of freely conducted research. Nor should it evolve as a function of the whims of parliamentary majorities. If judges are not supposed to write history, nor do parliaments have the vocation of legislating the past and fixing historical truth by vote. A nation should recognize its victims, that is, the victims of the crimes perpetrated in its name, and this recognition sometimes requires recourse to the law (such as the opening of archives). But the legislature should not go beyond its prerogatives. Recognition of the responsibility of the French state in the Vichy era for the deportation of Jews to the Nazi extermination camps, as admitted by Jacques Chirac at the start of his presidential term in 1995, was unanimously welcomed as a necessary act. Without being a law, this had a powerful effect.

Alongside civil religions, there is a memory that can be described as 'libertarian' or 'marrano', an unofficial memory, subterranean, transmitted outside of and often against the law. The memory of revolutions is subversive and critical when it inspires movements that challenge the established order. Under Stalinism, the commemoration of October 1917 became the liturgy of a political religion, the ritual of a totalitarian regime. The memory of the Holocaust was also a 'marrano' memory. In the 1950s and early 1960s, memory of the Nazi camps was an important lever, in France and elsewhere, to mobilize a section of the left and the intellectual world against the war in Algeria. Historical knowledge of the Judeocide was still very fragmentary at that time, but the meaning of the event, and the moral and political obligations that followed from it, were beyond doubt. This memory did not ask for laws; instead it led to the transgression of existing laws, for example by inspiring the *porteurs de valises*[29] or the signatories of the Manifesto of the 121 who called on soldiers to refuse to fight in a colonial war.

In 1965, Jean Améry published *At the Mind's Limits*, in which he related his experience as a Jew and Resistance fighter deported to Auschwitz. At the heart of his reflection, torture appeared not as a secondary aspect of Nazism but as 'its essence'. Of course, the Nazis did not invent torture, but they brought it to its apogee; it was in torture, Améry wrote, 'that the Third Reich materialized in all the density of its being'.[30] Often interpreted as a timeless meditation on violence, Améry's book is hard to understand outside its historical context. His bitter reflections on the ineffaceable character of the offence inflicted have a clear political dimension, and relate to the anti-colonial struggle that was current at the time that he published. His text resonates with Henri Alleg's *La question* (1958), which he himself quotes when he seeks to show that the violence that Nazism embodied between 1933 and 1945 was being continued during the Algerian war in the form of colonialism.[31]

Read today, these words of an Austrian Jew deported to Auschwitz read strangely. How can the experience of genocide be reduced to torture? The gas chambers and the cremation ovens stand at a different degree in the scale of abominations of the human species. No matter how touched the reader may be, Améry's lines seem inadequate and inappropriate. In the early 1960s, however, when Améry was writing, Auschwitz was not yet the paradigm of a rupture of civilization. The Holocaust was seen rather through the prism of colonialism, as the Algerian war was coming to an end and the US intervention in Vietnam was beginning. In this context, it seemed incongruous to consider a special event, historically singular and not reducible to the violence of imperialism – a violence which, for its part, continued the legacy of Nazism. The hermeneutic that inspired Améry's essay was eminently political. His testimony was not an exercise sufficient in itself; it was conceived as an act of combat. Fifty years later his book shows its limitations, its myopia, but also its strength: memory finds its meaning and utility in a radical critique of the injustices of the present. This is the exact opposite of the civil religion of the Holocaust, which erects a cult of the past by disassociating it from the present. As the result of a long historical process whose gestation took decades, it coincided with the end of communism and the defeat of the twentieth-century revolutions. Memory has lost its critical potential; it has become a monument.

Narcissistic compassion

It would be hard to maintain today that the commemoration of the liberation of Auschwitz in January 2005, with the participation in the front row of such architects of the invasion of Iraq as Dick Cheney, Jack Straw and Silvio Berlusconi, was a critical use of the memory of the Shoah. In January 2007, the French philosopher André Glucksmann published in *Le Monde* an op-ed piece entitled, 'Why I Choose Nicolas Sarkozy', in which he explained that the memory of the Holocaust lay at the root of his support for the right-wing candidate in the presidential election. 'Sarkozy's politics,' he wrote, are inspired by 'the murmur of innocent souls' he had heard at Yad Vashem, and since 'it has always been this murmur that supports [his] philosophy', he was the only candidate Glucksmann could vote for.[32] Crassly instrumentalized in this way, the critical potential of remembrance is demolished once and for all.

For Rousseau, civil religion was supposed to strengthen the solidarity of a collectivity solicitous of the common good. It aimed at the future rather than looking back on the past. The interest of history was as *magistra vitae*, not as a cult of the past cut off from the present. The present division of labour in the governments of the European Union, however, entrusts one ministry with the commemoration of victims while another plans raids and expulsions of illegal immigrants, revealing an ambiguity that risks wrong-footing the political virtues of memory. Conceived in order to fill a compensatory role – symbolic reparation for the wrongs of Europe and ending a long repression – the civil religion of the Holocaust seems to ignore any preventative aim: that it should never be repeated. When detention centres for illegal immigrants proliferate and governments organize their massive expulsion (sometimes on an ethnic basis, as with the Roms in France), a civil religion of the Holocaust impervious to this reality risks appearing as a diversion. It gives the impression of an enormous mechanism designed to protect the memory of a minority no longer threatened, in a context of collective indifference to those forms of oppression that really do exist in the present.

We can understand in this light the tormented observation of Peter Novick, who, at the end of his study on the memory of the Holocaust in the United States, points out its character as conformist, rhetorical, banal, inconsistent and above all depoliticized.[33] Europe cultivated anti-Semitism for centuries, without doing anything to prevent its expansion and radicalization in the twentieth century, leading to an epilogue of extermination. Now it deploys a considerable energy to preserve the memory of its crimes, at a time when those who suffered these are no longer threatened. To commemorate the victims of Nazi crimes is not a commitment to anything, especially if such commemorations do not aim to combat today's forms of xenophobia and exclusion. The integration of Jews into Western societies promotes an identification with their suffering that would have been inconceivable at the time they were a stigmatized minority. It is the same narcissistic compassion that moved the West at the moment of the attacks of 11 September 2001 ('We are all Americans'), when the victims of the World Trade Center aroused an emotion never shown for the Palestinians, Iraqis, Afghans or Tutsis.[34] Institutionalized and neutralized, the memory of the Holocaust thus risks becoming the moral sanction for a Western order that perpetuates oppression and injustice. Jewish modernity put an end to the liturgy of the memory of traditional Jewish communities and heralded an epoch of liberatory struggles inscribed in history — a common history. This modernity was obliterated in Auschwitz; the civil religion of the Holocaust is simply its epitaph.

Conclusion

In 1970, Isaiah Berlin sketched a parallel portrait of Benjamin Disraeli and Karl Marx. Beyond their worldviews, their political conceptions, their social conditions and even their opposite styles of life, he observed, Queen Victoria's prime minister and the exiled revolutionary had one thing in common. They were Jewish 'outsiders' who did not accept a place on the margin but nourished grand ambitions: 'the former saw himself as a natural leader of an aristocratic elite, and the latter as the teacher and strategist of the world proletariat'.[1] The one sought acceptance within the prevailing order and became one of its representatives, the other sought to destroy it; the one chose power, the other the radical critique of power, in both theory and practice. Sir Isaiah Berlin's sympathies were certainly with the British aristocrat, but the conservative historian was a subtle mind and his observations are not without finesse. The destinies of Disraeli and Marx reflect the dilemmas that tore modern intellectuals in their relationship with state power. They also reflect two distinct trajectories of the Jewish intelligentsia. If the model of critical intellectual embodied by Marx dominated the twentieth century, that of Disraeli became more general at the century's end, when revolutionaries gave way to statesmen and *consiglieri*. Today, the Jewish intellectual is no longer the pariah described by Hannah Arendt in the 1940s; he or she is rather to be found in think-tanks linked to the state, an 'organic intellectual' of the ruling classes. This shift is evidence of a change of era: the end of the age of critical Judaism and the beginning of that of a Judaism of order. Of course, these are not monolithic categories, and there are paths between the two; critical Jewry has not disappeared, and the Jewry of order is not the only one visible. What we see is a tendency opposed to one that took shape over the centuries, but this tendency is clear enough despite its contradictions, when Jewish history is regarded over the long term.

We can try to grasp this shift with the concept of 'recognition' that has lain at the heart of a rich philosophical and political debate in recent years. According to Nancy Fraser, a theory of justice appropriate for the issues of the contemporary world must tackle two central and indissociable questions: on the one hand, the social inequalities arising from class hierarchies and the socio-economic structures of domination; on the other hand, the denial of recognition – not only social, but also cultural and symbolic – suffered by whole layers of the population as a function of their exploitation, their ethnic or religious adherence or their gender identity.[2] These forms of oppression are not necessarily bound up with economic status or even legal discrimination; they concern individuals who fall more under the Weberian category of an 'order' (*Stand*) than under the Marxist category of class. However, if social inequality can only be eliminated by policies that attack property and proceed to a division of wealth, recognition implies a challenge to the dominant system of values. And just as a mere redistribution of incomes does not necessarily attack the sources of exploitation, simply limiting the effects of this, so too an identity policy that accepts differences can bring substantial gains in terms of rights and liberties, but does not for all that mean the end of prejudices, stereotypes and cultural hierarchies. Authentic recognition should thus go beyond the valuing of identities and alterities that were previously despised, to aim, in Fraser's words, at 'a complete transformation of societal models of representation', so that 'the identity of all is affected'.[3]

In historical terms, after emancipation (and in many parts of Europe even before) the 'Jewish question' was always bound up not with socio-economic equality but rather a denial of recognition. The social discrimination against Jews, wherever this was manifested (for example, their exclusion from public office), was a function of anti-Semitism, thus of symbolic contempt for them, rather than of the system of production. In the 1930s, the challenge by fascist regimes to the legal protections granted by emancipation transformed a stigmatized minority into a category of pariahs exposed to discrimination and persecution, culminating in extermination during the war. A vast literature has illustrated the identity-based suffering bound up with this denial of recognition. As witness, in the late sixteenth century, Shylock's famous monologue in *The Merchant of Venice*: 'Hath not a Jew eyes? Hath not a Jew hands, organs, dimensions, senses, affections, passions...' Or again, the reflections of Theodor Herzl, founder of Zionism, for whom the innocence of Captain Dreyfus was explained by the long history of humiliations that had aroused in Jews 'a pathological thirst for honours'.[4] Political Zionism, Leo Strauss emphasized in connection with Herzl, was concerned primarily with 'cleansing the Jews of their millennial degradation, with the recovery of Jewish dignity, honour and pride'.[5] And again, Hannah Arendt's autobiographical reflection in her lecture on the occasion of winning the Lessing prize in 1959: 'In this connection I cannot gloss over the fact that for many years I considered the only adequate reply to the question, Who are you? To be: A Jew. That answer alone took into account the reality of persecution.'[6]

The metamorphoses of the 'Jewish question' after the Shoah follow precisely from the end of this symbolic contempt and lack of recognition in a world in which neither social hierarchies nor structures of domination have been changed. Along the lines of other minority identities – homosexuals, blacks, etc. – Jewish alterity has ceased to be stigmatized in the public sphere and the dominant culture, where its expression has become legitimate or even a sign of distinction in the context of the valuing of multiculturalism. This gives rise to a 'particularist ethos' sustained by identification with the sufferings endured throughout history.[7] But the end of anti-Semitism does not mean the end of racism. The present book has shown how after the Second World War hatred of the Jews gave way to Islamophobia. The old prejudice even underwent a complete reversal since, as we have seen, the formerly stigmatized minority now occupies a quite unique position in the memories of the Western world. Its sufferings are proclaimed and the object of legal protection, as if Jews had always to be subject to special legislation, even if this is now in the form of positive discrimination. The shift from the stigmatization of Jewishness to its valorization thus promotes a movement of Jews into the structures of domination. Hence the transition within Jewish culture indicated above, from the intellectual pariah to the intellectual of power, from Marx to Disraeli. This switch could be interpreted in the light of the young Marx's essay on the Jewish question, once anachronistic readings and sterile polemics about its Jewish emancipation are jettisoned. Against Bruno Bauer, Marx called for the emancipation of Jews, but hastened to add that this would not be enough, since what was needed was universal emancipation.[8] Recognition without emancipation, however, can produce conformism.

CONCLUSION

One of the first attempts to explain the crucial position occupied by the Jews within modern culture goes back to the years that followed the First World War. In 1919, in an article that became classic, the sociologist Thorstein Veblen tried to explain why Jews had contributed more than any other group to the intellectual life of modern Europe. To his mind, the secret of their intellectual vitality lay in their status as 'a nation of hybrids', that is, assimilated Jews (they received a great deal of 'non-Jewish blood' in the course of their history).[9] According to Veblen, this 'hybrid' status removed them from the surrounding conformism and stimulated an attitude of scepticism that is the basis of science, discovery, the progress of knowledge. By identifying with all avant-garde currents they became 'pioneers', a kind of 'guild of enlighteners and iconoclasts'.[10] Valorizing the diaspora character of Jews at the time when the Versailles conference was fragmenting Europe into a mosaic of nation-states implied defining them as 'outsiders'. These were the people who created the Jewish golden age: writers outside the academy, bohemian artists, producers of ideas excluded from scientific institutions, critical intellectuals who straddled national divisions, cosmopolitan revolutionaries, heretics excommunicated by their own party (or religion). Recognition of Jewish alterity freed those who embodied this from their 'outsider' status, but also suppressed the premises of their anti-conformism. Critical thought remained a Jewish tradition, but ceased to be one of the 'negative privileges' that, according to Max Weber, characterized the Jewish condition. It is hard to imagine Kafka receiving a literary prize, Benjamin joining the Collège de France or the Max Planck Institut or Trotsky standing as a candidate in an election. We have already seen how the Americanization of Hannah Arendt, in other words the end of her condition as pariah intellectual, inflected the trajectory of her thought.

In the age of globalization of markets, knowledge and cultures, the advantages of diasporas tend to become normal structural conditions of all intellectual production. While Pierre Nora seeks to rescue French identity, it is an Indian, a West Indian and a Palestinian who have developed the concepts of 'hybridity' (Bhabha), 'creolization' (Glissant) and 'travelling theory' (Said).[11] But each diaspora is singular. European Jewish thought adopted a self-reflexive posture of Western culture, challenged from within by a stratum of its own representatives who, rejected and thrust to its margins, became its critical conscience (sometimes at the price of ignoring the non-European world, as in the case of the Frankfurt School and psychoanalysis). All these Jewish 'outsiders' displayed a deep and often tragic sense of belonging to Europe. It was in this sense that Kafka defined himself as a representative of the 'Western-Jewish age' (*westjüdische Zeit*),[12] and Hannah Arendt imagined Walter Benjamin lost in America as 'the last European'.[13]

Bhabha, Glissant and Said adopted a standpoint external to the European tradition. The starting point of post-colonialism lies in a critique of the Eurocentrism that may very well arise from Western culture itself – after all, its representatives are well established in American and British universities, which is something substantially different from the pariah Jewish intellectuals analysed in this book – but they view the world with the eyes of those whom Europe has always considered 'peoples without history'. The birth of post-colonialism coincides with the exhaustion of the Jewish cycle of critical thought in Europe, a few generations removed from the Holocaust and decolonization, when the cumulative effects of these two historical caesuras have become evident. The last work of Edward Said – an attempt to rescue humanism by a critical renewal[14] – could be read, from this point of view, as a dialogue between these two currents, written by an intellectual who was conscious of the richness of the Jewish tradition, by which he was himself deeply marked, and who sought to inject this into a new critical theory of domination. This is the meaning of the paradox that led him, in an interview with the Israeli newspaper *Haaretz*, to present himself as 'the last Jewish intellectual'.[15]

Notes

Introduction

1. Isaac Deutscher, *The Prophet Armed: Trotsky 1879–1921*, London: Verso, 2003, p. 299.
2. Quoted in Martin Gilbert, *Winston S. Churchill, Four: The Stricken World 1917–1922*, London: Heinemann, 1977, pp. 227–8.
3. John Maynard Keynes, *Two Memoirs: Dr Melchior, a Defeated Enemy. My Early Beliefs*, London: Rupert Hart-Davis, 1949, p. 61.
4. Cf. Christopher Hitchens, *The Trial of Henry Kissinger*, London: Verso, 2001.
5. Henry Kissinger, *Diplomacy*, New York: Simon & Schuster, 1994, p. 121.
6. Pierre Vidal-Naquet, *L'affaire Audin* (1958), Paris: Éditions de Minuit, 1989.
7. Boris Frankel and Sonia Combe, *Profession révolutionnaire*, Lormont: Au Bord de l'eau, 2004.
8. Jakob Moneta, *Mehr Gewalt für die Ohnmächtigen*, Frankfurt: ISP Verlag, 1991.
9. Yosef Hayim Yerushalmi, *Transmettre l'histoire juive. entretiens avec Sylvie Anne Goldberg*, Paris: Albin Michel, 2012, p. 45.

Chapter 1

1. Dan Diner, 'Einführung', in *Enzyklopädie jüdischer Geschichte und Kultur*, Stuttgart: J. B. Metzler, vol. 1, pp. 8–9.
2. Among a wide variety of sources, cf. in particular H. Stuart Hughes, *The Sea Change: The Migration of Social Thought 1930–1965*, New York: McGraw Hill, 1975.
3. Cf. Bernard Wasserstein, *Vanishing Diaspora: The Jews in Europe Since 1945*, London: Hamish Hamilton, 1996, p. viii.
4. Ibid., p. 92.
5. Yosef Hayim Yerushalmi, *Zakhor: Jewish History and Jewish Memory*, Seattle: University of Washington Press, 1982, p. 85.
6. Cf. Shmuel Feiner, *The Jewish Enlightenment*, Philadelphia: University of Pennsylvania Press, 2004.
7. Yosef Hayim Yerushalmi, *Freud's Moses: Judaism Terminable and Interminable*, New Haven: Yale University Press, 1993, p. 78.

8. Natan Sznaider, *Jewish Memory and Cosmopolitan Order: Hannah Arendt and the Jewish Condition*, Cambridge: Polity, 2011, p. 21.
9. Quoted in Patrick Girard, *La révolution française et les juifs*, Paris: Robert Laffont, 1989, p. 125.
10. Jacob Katz, 'A State Within a State: The History of an Anti-Semitic Slogan', in *Zur Assimilation und Emanzipation der Juden*, Darmstadt: Wissenschaftliche Buchgesellschaft, 1982, pp. 124–53.
11. Cf. Régine Robin, *L'amour du Yiddish. Écriture juive et sentiment de la langue 1830–1930*, Paris: Éditions du Sorbier, 1984; Rachel Ertel, *Le shtetl. La bourgade juive de Pologne*, Paris: Payot, 1986; and Emanuel Goldsmith, *Modern Yiddish Language: The Story of the Yiddish Language Movement*, New York: Fordham, 1988.
12. Simon Dubnov, *Judaism and History: Essays on Old and New Judaism*, Philadelphia: Jewish Publication Society, 1958.
13. Arno Mayer, *The Persistence of the Old Regime: Europe to the Great War*, London: Verso, 2010.
14. Dan Diner, *Gedächtniszeiten. Über jüdische und andere Geschichten*, Munich: C. H. Beck, 2013, p. 13; Tony Judt and Timothy Snyder, *Thinking the Twentieth Century*, New York: Penguin, 2012, p. 19. On the imperial structures of the nineteenth century, see in particular Jürgen Osterhammel, *Die Verwandlung der Welt. Eine Geschichte des 19. Jahrhunderts*, Munich: C. H. Beck, 2009, pp. 603–45, especially his 'ideal type' definition of empires, pp. 615–16.
15. Yosef Hayim Yerushalmi, *Serviteurs des rois et non serviteurs des serviteurs. sur quelques aspects de l'histoire politique des juifs*, Paris: Allia, 2011, p. 29.
16. Cf. David Biale, *Power and Powerlessness in Jewish History*, New York: Schocken, 1986, pp. 90–1.
17. Cf. Esther Benbassa, *Histoire des juifs de France*, Paris: Le Seuil, 1997, p. 164.
18. Cf. Werner Mosse, *The Jews in the German Economy: The German-Jewish Economic Elite 1820–1935*, New York: OUP, 1987; Yehudah Don and Victor Karady (ed.), *A Social and Economic History of Central European Jewry*, New Brunswick: Transaction, 1990. For an overall view, cf. Victor Karady, *The Jews of Europe in the Modern Era*, Budapest: Central European University Press, 2001, ch. 1.
19. Dan Diner, 'Ambiguous Semantics: Reflections on Jewish Political Concepts', *Jewish Quarterly Review*, vol. 98, no. 1, 2008, pp. 89–102.
20. Ernest Renan, 'Histoire générale et système comparé des langues sémitiques', *Oeuvres complètes*, vol. 8, Paris: Calmann-Lévy, 1967, p. 55. Cf. Shlomo Sand, *On the Nation and the 'Jewish People'*, London: Verso, 2010.

21. Arnold Toynbee, *A Study of History*, New York: OUP, 1947, vol. 1, pp. 388–9. Cf. Stéphane Dufoix, *La dispersion. Une histoire des usages du mot diaspora*, Paris: Éditions Amsterdam, 2011, pp. 175–80.
22. Cf. Heinrich Graetz, *History of the Jews* (5 vols), London, 1891–92. Simon Doubnov, *Histoire moderne du peuple juif 1789–1938*, Paris: Éditions du Cerf, 1994.
23. Shlomo Sand, *The Invention of the Jewish People*, London: Verso, 2009.
24. Gabriel Piterberg, *The Returns of Zionism: Myths, Politics and Scholarship in Israel*, London: Verso, 2008, chs 6 and 7.
25. Hannah Arendt, 'The Jew as Pariah: A Hidden Tradition', in *The Jewish Writings*, New York: Schocken, 2008. On the history of this notion, see in particular Arnaldo Momigliano, 'Considerazioni sulla definizione weberiana del giudaismo come religion paria', *Pagine ebraiche*, Turin: Einaudi, 1987, pp. 181–8 and Enzo Traverso, *The Jews and Germany: From the 'Judeo-German Symbiosis' to the Memory of Auschwitz*, Lincoln: University of Nebraska Press, 1995, ch. 2.
26. *The Sociology of George Simmel* (trans. and ed. Kurt H. Wolff), New York: The Free Press, 1964, pp. 402–8; Moische Postone, 'Nationalsozialismus und Antisemitismus. Ein theoretisher Versucht', in Dan Diner (ed.), *Zivilisationsbruch. Denken nach Auschwitz*, Frankfurt: Fischer, 1988, pp. 242–54.
27. Jeffrey Herf, *Reactionary Modernism: Technology, Culture, and Politics in Weimar and the Third Reich*, New York: CUP, 1984.
28. Cf. Enzo Traverso, *The Origins of Nazi Violence*, New York: New Press, 2003, ch. 5. Saul Friedländer, *Nazi Germany and the Jews, 1933–1945*, London: Phoenix, 2014, ch. 3.
29. On Vladimir Medem and his critique of the idea of a 'world Jewish nation', cf. Enzo Traverso, *The Marxists and the Jewish Question*, Atlantic Highlands: Humanities Press, 1994, pp. 100–10.
30. Dean Silvers, 'The Future of International Law as Seen Through the Jewish Material Claims Against Germany', *Jewish Social Studies*, vol. 42, no. 3–4, 1980, pp. 215–28. On the history of the Claims Conference, cf. Marilyn Henry, *Confronting the Perpetrators: A History of the Claims Conference*, London: Vallentine Mitchell, 2007 and Dan Diner and Gotthart Wunberg (ed.), *Restitution and Memory: Material Restoration in Europe*, New York: Berghahn, 2007.
31. Émile Durkheim, *On Suicide* (1897), Penguin: London, 2007, p. 405.
32. Tony Judt, *Postwar: A History of Europe Since 1945*, London: Vintage, 2010, p. 157.
33. Quoted in Ella Shohat, *Le sionisme du point de vue de ses victimes juives. Les juifs orientaux en Israël*, Paris: La Fabrique, 2006, pp. 44–5.

34. Fritz Stern, *Gold and Iron: Bismarck, Bleichröder, and the Building of the German Empire*, London: Allen and Unwin, 1977. Henri Raczymov, 'Proust et la judéité. Les destins croisés de Swann et Bloch', in *Ruse et déni. cinq essais de littérature*, Paris: PUF, 2011, pp. 65–98.
35. Régis Debray, À un ami israélien (with a response by Élie Barnavi), Paris: Flammarion, 2010, p. 42.
36. Günther Anders, 'Mein Judentum' (1978), in *Das Günther Anders Lesebuch*, Zurich, 1984, pp. 242–3.
37. Alexis de Tocqueville, *Democracy in America* (ed. Euardo Nolla), Indianapolis: Liberty Fund, 2010, vol. I, p. 418.
38. Yerushalmi, *Serviteurs des rois*, p. 78.
39. Diner, *Gedächtniszeiten*, p. 14.
40. Wasserstein, *Vanishing Diaspora*, p. vii.
41. Gershom Scholem (ed.), *The Correspondence of Walter Benjamin and Gershom Scholem*, New York: Schocken, 1989, p. 265.
42. On the history of this concept of German origin (*Judenfrage*), cf. Jacob Toury, 'The Jewish Question: A Semantic Approach', *Leo Baeck Institute Year Book*, 1996, New York: OUP, vol. 11, pp. 85–106 and Axel Bein, *Die Judenfrage. Biographie eines Weltproblems* (2 vols), Stuttgart: Deutsche Verlags-Anstalt, 1980.
43. Theodor Herzl, *The Jewish State* (1896), London: Penguin, 2010, p. 31.
44. Karl Marx, 'On the Jewish Question', in *Marx Engels Collected Works*, vol. 3, London: Lawrence & Wishart, 1975, pp. 146–74; Abraham Léon, *La conception matérialiste de la question juive*, Paris: EDI, 1980; Jean-Paul Sartre, 'Reflections on the Jewish Question' (1946), *October*, vol. 87, winter 1999, pp. 32–46.
45. Pierre Nora, 'Between Memory and History', in *Realms of Memory: The Reconstruction of the French Past, I. Conflicts and Divisions* (ed. Pierre Nora), New York: Columbia University Press, 1996, pp. 1–21.
46. Pierre Nora, *Présent, nation, mémoire*, Paris: Gallimard, 2011, p. 386.

Chapter 2

1. See George K. Anderson, *The Myth of the Wandering Jew*, New York: Brown, 1965; Edgar Knecht, *Le mythe du juif errant. Essai de mythologie littéraire et de sociologie religieuse*, Grenoble: Presses universitaires de Grenoble, 1977; and the essays collected in the catalogue of the exhibition of the Musée d'Art et d'Histoire du Judaïsme, *Le juif errant. Un témoin du temps*, Paris: Adam Biro, 2001.
2. Cf. Natan Sznaider, *Jewish Memory and Cosmopolitan Order: Hannah Arendt and the Jewish Condition*, Cambridge: Polity Press, 2011, p. 1.

3. Samuel Joseph, *Jewish Immigration to the United States from 1881 to 1910*, New York: AMS Press, pp. 117, 120.
4. Cf. Jacques Le Rider, *La Mitteleuropa*, Paris: PUF, 1994.
5. Cf. Otto Bauer, *The Question of Nationalities and Social Democracy*, Ann Arbor: University of Minnesota Press, 2000. It should be remembered that Bauer, the author of this formula, refused to apply it to the Jews.
6. Cf. David Sorkin, 'Emancipation and Assimilation: Two Concepts and their Application to German-Jewish History', *Leo Baeck Institute Year Book*, New York: OUP, vol. 35, 1990, pp. 17–33. On this problematic as a whole, see also George L. Mosse, *German Jews Beyond Judaism*, Bloomington: Indiana University Press and Jacques Ehrenfreund, *Mémoire juive et nationalité allemande. Les juifs berlinois à la Belle époque*, Paris: PUF, 2000.
7. Hermann Cohen, 'Deutschtum und Judentum' (1915), in Christoph Schulte (ed.), *Deutschtum und Judentum. Ein Disput unter Juden aus Deutschland*, Stuttgart: Reclam, 1993, pp. 40–69.
8. Cf. Michael Graetz, 'The History of an Estrangement Between Two Jewish Communities: German and French Jewry During the Nineteenth Century', in Jacob Katz (ed.), *Toward Modernity: The European Jewish Model*, New Brunswick: Transaction, pp. 159–69 and Herbert Lottman, *La dynastie Rothschild*, Paris: Le Seuil, 1994, p. 72.
9. Cf. Jacob Katz, *Hors du ghetto. L'emancipation des juifs en Europe*, Paris: Hachette, 1984.
10. Cf. Michel Espagne, *Les juifs allemands de Paris à l'époque de Heine. La translation ashkénaze*, Paris: PUF, 1996.
11. Cf. Peter Pulzer, *The Rise of Political Anti-Semitism in Germany and Austria*, Cambridge, MA: Harvard University Press, 1988; Helmut Berding, *Moderner Antisemitismus in Deutschland*, Frankfurt: Suhrkampf, 1988 and Massimo Ferrari Zumbini, *Die Wurzeln des Bösen. Gründerjahre des Antisemitismus von Bismarckzeit bis Hitler*, Frankfurt: Klosterman, 2003.
12. Cf. Sergio Della Pergola, *Le trasformazioni demografiche della diaspora ebraica*, Turin: Loescher, 1983, p. 100; Marsha Rozenblit, *The Jews of Vienna 1867–1914: Assimilation and Identity*, Albany: State University of New York Press, 1983, ch. 2; Steven Beller, *Vienna and the Jews 1867–1938: A Cultural History*, Cambridge: CUP, 1989, ch. 3; Uri Kaufmann, 'Sozial- und Wirtschaftsstruktur der jüdischen Gemeinden', in Elke-Vera Kotowski, Julius Schoeps and Hiltrud Wallenborn (ed.), *Handbuch zur Geschichte der Juden in Europa*, Darmstadt: Wissenschaftliche Buchgesellschaft, 2001, Bd. 2, pp. 48–57.

13. Cf. Ulrich Engelhardt, *'Bildungsbürgertum'. Begriffs- und Dogmengeschichte eines Etiketts*, Stuttgart: Klett-Cotta, 1986. On Jews of this social stratum, see Shulamit Volkov, *Jüdisches Leben und Antisemitismus im 19. und 20. Jahrhundert*, Munich: C. H. Beck, 1990, chs 6 and 7 and, by the same author, *Das jüdische Projekt der Moderne*, Munich: C. H. Beck, 2001, ch. 7.
14. Cf. Aleida Assmann, *Construction de la mémoire nationale. Une brève histoire de l'idée allemande de Bildung*, Paris: Éditions de la Maison des sciences de l'homme, 1994.
15. Cf. Pierre Birnbaum, *Les fous de la République. histoire politique des juifs d'État de Gambetta à Vichy*, Paris: Fayard, 1992.
16. Cf. Pierre Birnbaum, *Un mythe politique. La 'République juive' de Léon Blum à Mendès France*, Paris: Fayard, 1988 and Zeev Sternhell, *La droite révolutionnaire. les origines françaises du fascisme*, Paris: Gallimard, 1997.
17. Norbert Elias, 'Notes on a Lifetime', in *Reflections on a Life*, Cambridge: Polity Press, 1994, pp. 81–154 (p. 121).
18. Moritz Goldstein, *Berliner Jahre. Erinnerungen 1880–1933*, Munich: Verlag Dokumentation, 1997, p. 221.
19. David Sorkin, *The Transformation of German Jewry 1780–1840*, New York: OUP, 1987.
20. Rachel Ertel, *Le shtetl. La bourgade juive de Pologne*, Paris: Payot, 1986.
21. Régine Robin, *L'amour du Yiddish. Écriture juive et sentiment de la langue 1830–1930*, Paris: Éditions du Sorbier, 1984, pp. 37–8.
22. Cf. Gershom Scholem, 'The Science of Judaism – Then and Now', in *The Messianic Idea in Judaism: And Other Essays on Jewish Spirituality*, New York: Schocken, 1995, pp. 304–13; Maurice-Ruben Hayoun, *Les lumières de Cordoue à Berlin. Une histoire intellectuelle du judaïsme* (2 vols), Paris: Lattès, 1996 and 1998, vol. 2.
23. Heinrich Graetz, *Construction de l'histoire juive*, Paris: Éditions du Cerf, 1992.
24. Perrine Simon-Nahum, *La cité investie. La 'Science du judaïsme' française et la République*, Paris: Éditions du Cerf, 1991.
25. George L. Mosse, 'Jewish Emancipation: Between *Bildung* and Respectability', in *Confronting the Nation: Jewish and Western Nationalism*, London: Brandeis University Press, 1993, pp. 131–45.
26. Shulamit Volkov, 'Antisemitismus als kultureller Code', in *Jüdisches Leben und Antisemitismus im 19. und 20. Jahrhundert*, pp. 13–35.
27. Hannah Arendt, 'Stefan Zweig: Jews in the World of Yesterday', in *The Jewish Writings*, New York: Schocken, 2008, p. 326.

28. Joseph Roth, 'Das autodafé des Geistes', in *Berliner Saisonbericht. Reportagen und journalistische Arbeiten (1920–1939)*, Cologne: Kiepenheuer & Witsch, 1984, pp. 389–90.
29. Karl Marx, 'On the Jewish Question', in *Marx Engels Collected Works*, vol. 3, London: Lawrence & Wishart, 1975, pp. 146–74.
30. Hannah Arendt, *The Origins of Totalitarianism*, London: Deutsch, 1986, p. 64.
31. Robert Michels, *Political Parties*, New York: Simon & Schuster, 1968, p. 247.
32. Abraham J. Karp, *Golden Door to America: The Jewish Experience*, New York: Viking Press, 1976, p. 202.
33. Cf. Enzo Traverso, *The Marxists and the Jewish Question*, Atlantic Highlands: Humanities Press, 1994, pp. 32–57. On Jewish and socialist cosmopolitanism in the tsarist empire, which maintained very close links with Germany in this respect, cf. Claudie Weill, *Les cosmopolites. Socialisme et judéité en Russie (1897–1917)*, Paris: Syllepse, 2004.
34. Eric Hobsbawm, 'Intellectuals and the Class Struggle', in *Revolutionaries: Contemporary Essays*, London: Weidenfeld & Nicolson, 1973.
35. *The Letters of Rosa Luxemburg* (ed. G. Adler, P. Hudis and A. Laschitza), London: Verso, 2011, p. 376.
36. Peter Gay, *Weimar Culture: The Outsider as Insider*, New York: Norton, 2001, p. 145.
37. Herbert Strauss, *Jewish Immigrants of the Nazi Period in the USA*, Munich: Saur, vol. 6, 1987, p. 151.
38. Jean-Michel Palmier, *Weimar in Exile*, London: Verso, 2004 and Horst Möller, *Exodus der Kultur. Schriftsteller, Wissenschaftler und Künstler in der Emigration nach 1933*, Munich: C. H. Beck, 1984.
39. Walter Benjamin, 'German Men and Women', in *Selected Writings, Volume 3, 1935–1938* (ed. Howard Eiland and Michael W. Jennings), Cambridge, MA: Harvard University Press, 2002, pp. 167–235.
40. Quoted in Albrecht Schöne, '"Diese nach jüdischen Vorbild erbaute Arche". Walter Benjamins Deutsche Menschen', in Stéphane Moses and Albrecht Schöne (ed.), *Juden in der deutschen Literatur*, Frankfurt: Suhrkamp, 1986, pp. 350–65 (p. 356).
41. Siegfried Kracauer, *Jacques Offenbach and the Paris of His Time*, Cambridge, MA: Zone Books, 2003.
42. Stefan Zweig, *The World of Yesterday*, Lincoln: University of Nebraska Press, 2013.
43. Joseph Roth, 'Panoptikum', in *Gesammelte Werke*, Bd. 3, Cologne: Kiepenheuer & Witsch, 1975, p. 568.

44. Cf. Hans-Dietrich Krohn, *Wissenschaft im Exil. Deutsche Sozial- und Wirtschafts-Wissenschaftler in den USA und die New School for Social Research*, Frankfurt: Campus, 1987.
45. H. Stuart Hughes, *The Sea Change: The Migration of Social Thought 1930–1965*, New York: Harper & Row, 1975.
46. Cf. George L. Mosse, 'The End is Not Yet: A Personal Memoir of the German-Jewish Legacy in America', in Abraham J. Peck (ed.), *The German-Jewish Legacy in America 1938–1988: From Bildung to the Bill of Rights*, Detroit: Wayne State University Press, 1989, pp. 11–18.
47. Karl Mannheim, 'The Function of the Refugee: A Rejoinder', *New English Weekly*, vol. 27, no. 1, 1945, pp. 5–6.

Chapter 3

1. Karl Marx, 'On the Jewish Question', in *Marx Engels Collected Works*, vol. 3, London: Lawrence & Wishart, 1975, pp. 146–74.
2. Yuri Slezkine, *Le siècle juif*, Paris: La Découverte, 2009, ch. 1.
3. Isaac Deutscher, 'The Non-Jewish Jew' (1958), in *The Non-Jewish Jew*, Oxford: OUP, 1968, p. 26.
4. David Biale, *Not in the Heavens: The Tradition of Jewish Secular Thought*, Princeton: Princeton University Press, 2011, pp. 9–10, 176.
5. Deutscher, 'The Non-Jewish Jew', pp. 33–4.
6. Ibid., p. 27.
7. *The Letters of Rosa Luxemburg* (ed. G. Adler, P. Hudis and A. Laschitza), London: Verso, 2011, p. 376.
8. Isaac Deutscher, 'Who Is a Jew?', in *The Non-Jewish Jew*, p. 47. See also Michael Löwy, *Rédemption et utopie: le judaïsme libertaire en Europe centrale*, Paris: PUF, 1988, pp. 54–61. On Deutscher's intellectual and political trajectory, cf. David Horowitz (ed.), *Isaac Deutscher: The Man and His Work*, London: Macdonald, 1971.
9. Deutscher, 'Who Is a Jew?', p. 49.
10. Ibid., p. 51.
11. Hannah Arendt, 'The Jew as Pariah: A Hidden Tradition', in *The Jewish Writings*, New York: Schocken, 2008. This notion will be discussed in Chapter 4.
12. Deutscher, 'The Non-Jewish Jew', p. 31.
13. Jean-Paul Sartre, 'Reflections on the Jewish Question: A Lecture', *October*, vol. 87, winter 1999, pp. 32–46.
14. Deutscher, 'Who Is a Jew?', p. 47.
15. See Daniel Lindenberg, *Figures d'Israël: l'identité juive entre marranisme et sionisme (1648–1998)*, Paris: Hachette, 1997.

16. Quoted by Yirmiyahu Yovel, *Spinoza et autres hérétiques*, Paris: Le Seuil, 1991, p. 65. See also Gabriel Albiac, *La synagogue vide. Les sources marranes du spinozisme*, Paris: PUF, 1994.
17. Cf. Jonathan I. Israel, *Les lumières radicales. la philosophie, Spinoza et la naissance de la modernité (1650–1750)*, Paris: Éditions Amsterdam, 2005.
18. Lindenberg, *Figures d'Israël*.
19. Jacob Katz, *Hors du ghetto. L'émancipation des juifs en Europe 1770–1870*, Paris: Hachette, 1984.
20. Pierre Birnbaum, *Les fous de la République. histoire politique des juifs d'État de Gambetta à Vichy*, Paris: Fayard, 1992.
21. Cf. Pierre Birnbaum, *Un mythe politique. La 'République juive' de Léon Blum à Mendès France*, Paris: Fayard, 1988.
22. Raymond Aron, *Memoirs: Fifty Years of Political Reflection*, Holmes & Meier, 1990, p. 336. See also Pierre Birnbaum, '"Un juif français authentique" à la recherche de ses racines', *Géographie de l'espoir. L'exil, les lumières, la désassimilation*, Paris: Gallimard, 2004, pp. 168–99.
23. Cf. Nicolas Baverez, *Raymond Aron*, Paris: Flammarion, 1993, pp. 395–6. ('*Chienlit*', literally 'bed-shitters', was the abusive term with which de Gaulle referred to the May 1968 demonstrators. – Translator.)
24. Antonio Gramsci, *Prison Notebooks, Volume 3*, New York: Columbia University Press, 1991; Arnaldo Momigliano, 'Gli ebrei d'Italia', in *Pagine ebraiche*, Turin: Einaudi, 1987, pp. 129–42. On Gramsci and Momigliano, see Francesca Sofia, 'Su assimilazione e autocoscienza ebraica nell'Italia liberale', *Il pensiero politico*, vol. 24, 1991, pp. 34–57 and Simon Levis Sullam, 'Arnaldo Momigliano e la "nazionalizzazione parallela": autobiografia, religione, storia', *Passato e Presente*, vol. 25, no. 70, 2007, pp. 59–82.
25. Momigliano, 'Gli ebrei d'Italia', p. 134.
26. Tullia Catalan, 'L'organizzazione delle comunità ebraiche italiane dall'Unità alla prima guerra mondiale', in Corrado Vivanti (ed.), *Storia d'Italia, Annali 11, Gli ebrei in Italia, t. 2, Dall'emancipazione a oggi*, Turin: Einaudi, 1997, p. 1267.
27. See Cesare Lombroso, *L'antisémitisme*, Paris: Giard et Brière, 1899.
28. Cf. Sander Gilman, *Jewish Self-hatred: Anti-Semitism and the Hidden Language of the Jews*, Baltimore: Johns Hopkins Press, 1986 and the classic essay by Theodor Lessing, *La haine de soi, ou le refus d'être juif* (1930), Paris: Berg International, 2001.
29. Cf. Alain Boureau, *Histoires d'un historien: Kantorowicz*, Paris: Gallimard, 1990.

30. Cf. Hans-Joachim Schoeps, 'Das neue Gesicht der Politik' (1933) and 'Der Deutsche Vortrupp, Gefolgschaft deutscher Juden' (1933), in *'Bereit für Deutschland': Der Patriotismus deutscher Juden und der National-Sozialismus, Frühe Schriften 1930–1939. Eine historische Dokumentation*, Berlin: Haude & Spener, 1970, pp. 69–95 and pp. 97–165.
31. Cf. Amos Elon, *The Pity of It All: A Portrait of the German-Jewish Epoch 1743–1933*, New York: Picador, 2002, pp. 315–17.
32. Walther Rathenau, 'Staat und Judentum' (1911), in *Gesammelte Schriften*, Berlin: Fischer, 1918, Bd. 1, pp. 188–9. See also Peter Loewenberg, *Walther Rathenau and Henry Kissinger: The Jew as a Modern Statesman in Two Political Cultures*, New York: Leo Baeck Memorial Lectures, 1980, p. 8.
33. Loewenberg, *Walther Rathenau and Henry Kissinger*, p. 16. Cf. also Peter Gay, *Freud, Jews and Other Germans: Masters and Victims in Modernist Culture*, Oxford: OUP, 1979, p. 197.
34. Cf. Bernard Glassman, *Benjamin Disraeli: The Fabricated Jew in Myth and Memory*, New York: OUP, 2003.
35. Loewenberg, *Walther Rathenau and Henry Kissinger*.
36. Cf. Gangolf Hübinger, *Gelehrte, Politik, und Öffentlichkeit. Eine Intellektuellengeschichte*, Göttingen: Vandenhoeck & Ruprecht, 2006.
37. Pierre Drieu La Rochelle, *Gilles* (1939), Paris: Gallimard, 1949, p. 100.
38. On the conflicts between nationalism and the 'new Sorbonne' at the turn of the century, cf. Wolf Lepenies, *Between Literature and Science: The Rise of Sociology*, Cambridge: CUP, 1988, pp. 47 ff.; on the Dreyfusard commitment of the Durkheimian school, cf. Ivan Strenski, *Durkheim and the Jews of France*, Chicago: University of Chicago Press, 1997 and Birnbaum, 'Emile David Durkheim: La mémoire de Masada', *Géographie de l'espoir*, pp. 85–123.
39. Marc Bloch, *L'histoire, la guerre, la Résistance*, Paris: Gallimard, 2006; Raymond Aron, 'Bergson' (1941), in *Essais sur la condition juive contemporaine*, Paris: Tallandier, 2007; Pierre Vidal-Naquet, *Mémoires 1. La brisure et l'attente 1930–1955*, Paris: Le Seuil/La Découverte, 1995, p. 102.
40. Raymond Aron, 'Face à la tragédie' (1967), in *Essais sur la condition juive contemporaine*, p. 127.
41. Elisabeth Roudinesco, *Revisiting the Jewish Question*, Cambridge: Polity, 2013, ch. 4.
42. Perry Anderson, 'L'union sucrée', *London Review of Books*, vol. 26, no. 18, 23 September 2004. Cf. Pierre Nora, 'Between Memory and History', in *Realms of Memory: The Reconstruction of the French Past, I. Conflicts and Divisions* (ed. Pierre Nora), New York: Columbia University Press,

1996, pp. 1–21. On the identity-based conservatism that inspired Nora's work, cf. Marcel Detienne, *L'identité nationale. Une énigme*, Paris: Gallimard, 2010.

43. Cf. Malachi H. Hacohen, 'From Empire to Cosmopolitanism: The Central European Jewish Intelligentsia, 1867–1968', *Jahrbuch des Simon-Dubnow-Instituts*, no. 5, 2006, pp. 117–33.

44. Cf. Peter Coleman, *The Cultural Conspiracy: The Congress for Cultural Freedom and the Struggle for the Mind in Postwar Europe*, New York: Free Press, 1989 and Pierre Grémion, *Intelligence de l'anticommunisme. Le Congrès pour la liberté de la culture à Paris (1950–1975)*, Paris: Fayard, 1995.

45. Salo W. Baron, *Social and Religious History of the Jews*, New York: Columbia University Press, vol. 2, 1937, p. 39.

46. Ibid., pp. 316–17. Cf. also Salo W. Baron, 'The Jewish Question in the Nineteenth Century', *Journal of Modern History*, vol. 10, no. 1, 1938, pp. 51–65. On Baron's Habsburg provenance, cf. David Engel, 'Crisis and Lachrimosity: On Salo Baron, Neobaronianism, and the Study of Modern European Jewish History', *Jewish History*, vol. 20, no. 3–4, 2006, pp. 243–64.

47. Quoted in Milton M. Gordon, *Assimilation in American Life: The Role of Race, Religion, and National Origins*, New York: OUP, 1964, p. 142.

48. Karl Popper, *The Open Society and Its Enemies, Volume 2, The High Tide of Prophecy: Hegel, Marx, and the Aftermath*, London: Routledge, 1962, esp. p. 63.

49. Ibid., p. 51. See Malachi H. Hacohen, *Karl Popper, the Formative Years, 1902–1945: Politics and Philosophy in Interwar Vienna*, New York: CUP, 2000.

50. Cf. Malachi H. Hacohen, '"The Strange Fact that Israel Exists": The Cold War Liberals Between Cosmopolitanism and Nationalism', *Jewish Social Studies, History, Culture, Society*, vol. 15, no. 2, 2009, pp. 37–81 (p. 58).

51. Isaiah Berlin, 'The Counter-Enlightenment', in *Against the Current: Essays in the History of Ideas* (1955), Princeton: Princeton University Press, 2013, pp. 15–16.

52. John Gray, *Berlin*, London: Fontana Press, 1999, p. 156.

53. Berlin, 'The Counter-Enlightenment'.

54. Isaiah Berlin, *The Magus of the North: J. G. Hamann and the Origins of Modern Irrationalism*, New York: Farrar, Straus & Giroux, 1994, pp. 106 and 71.

55. Jacob Talmon, *The Origins of Totalitarian Democracy*, London: Secker & Warburg, 1960.

56. Isaiah Berlin, *Freedom and Its Betrayal: Six Enemies of Human Liberties*, London: Chatto & Windus, 2002, p. 49.
57. Zeev Sternhell, *The Anti-Enlightenment Tradition*, New Haven: Yale University Press, p. 373.
58. Quoted in Michael Ignatieff, *Isaiah Berlin: A Life*, London: Vintage, 1998, p. 283.
59. Cf. Tariq Ali, *The Clash of Fundamentalisms: Crusades, Jihads and Modernity*, London: Verso, 2003, p. 128.
60. Cf. Ignatieff, *Isaiah Berlin*, p. 283.
61. Ivan Segré, 'The Philo-Semitic Reaction: The Treason of the Intellectuals', in Alain Badiou, Eric Hazan and Ivan Segré (ed.), *Reflections on Anti-Semitism*, London: Verso, 2013, pp. 45–241 (p. 47).
62. Cf. Shadia Drury, *The Political Ideas of Leo Strauss*, New York: Palgrave, 2005. See also Daniel Tanguy, *Leo Strauss. Une biographie intellectuelle*, Paris: Grasset, 2003.
63. See in particular Leo Strauss, 'Introduction', in *Spinoza's Critique of Religion*, Chicago: Chicago University Press, 1997. Also on this subject, Pierre Bouretz, 'Leo Strauss devant la modernité juive', *Raisons politiques*, vol. 4, no. 8, 2002, pp. 33–60.
64. Leo Strauss, 'Progress or Return?', in *The Rebirth of Classical Political Rationalism*, Chicago: University of Chicago Press, 1989, pp. 227–69. See also Leo Strauss, 'Jerusalem and Athens: Some Preliminary Reflections' (1967), in *Studies in Platonic Political Philosophy*, Chicago: University of Chicago Press, 1985, pp. 147–73.
65. Cf. Anne Norton, *Leo Strauss and the Politics of American Empire*, New Haven: Yale University Press, 2005, pp. 201–9. On the genesis of the neoconservative Straussian current, cf. Shadia Drury, *Leo Strauss and the American Right*, New York: Palgrave, 1999. On the Jewish contribution to the neoconservative right, cf. Murray Friedman, *The Neoconservative Revolution: Jewish Intellectuals and the Shaping of Public Policy*, New York: CUP, 2005 and Klaus J. Milch, 'Fundamentalism Hot and Cold: George W. Bush and the "Return of the Sacred"', *Cultural Critique*, no. 62, 2006, pp. 92–125. On the convergence between the different elements of the American conservative right, cf. Alain Frachon and Daniel Vernet, *L'Amérique des néoconservateurs. l'illusion messianique*, Paris: Perrin, 2010 and Wendy Brown, *Les habits neufs de la politique mondiale. néolibéralisme et néoconservatisme*, Paris: Les Prairies ordinaires, 2007.
66. Cf. Hans J. Morgenthau, 'Fragment of an Intellectual Autobiography', in Kenneth Thompson and Robert Myers (ed.), *Truth and Tragedy: A Tribute to Hans J. Morgenthau*, New Brunswick: Transaction, 1984, pp. 1–17;

Alfons Söller, 'German Conservatism in America: Morgenthau's Political Realism', *Telos*, no. 72, 1987, pp. 161–72.
67. Samuel Huntington, *The Clash of Civilizations and the Remaking of World Order*, New York: Simon & Shuster, 1993.
68. Cf. in particular Shadia Drury, 'Straussians in Power: Secrecy, Lies, and Endless War', in *The Political Ideas of Leo Strauss*, pp. ix–lix. See also John G. Mason, 'Guerre d'Irak et guerre culturelle. Les "pieux mensonges" néoconservateurs', *Critique*, no. 682, 2004/3, pp. 191–208.
69. Robert Kagan, *Of Paradise and Power: America and Europe in the New World Order*, New York: Vintage, 2004.
70. Allan Bloom, *The Closing of the American Mind: How Higher Education Has Failed Democracy and Impoverished the Souls of Today's Students*, New York: Simon & Shuster, 1988.
71. See Alan M. Wald, *The New York Intellectuals: The Rise and Fall of the Anti-Stalinist Left from the 1930s to the 1980s*, Chapel Hill: University of North Carolina Press, 1987.
72. Franco Fortini, *I cani del Sinai*, Bari: De Donato, 1967, p. 26.
73. Daniel Lindenberg, *Le rappel à l'ordre. enquête sur les nouveaux réactionnaires*, Paris: Le Seuil, 2002.
74. Quoted in Arno J. Mayer, *Ploughshares into Swords: From Zionism to Israel*, London: Verso, 2008, pp. 81–2.
75. Norbert Elias, 'Notes on a Lifetime', in *Reflections on a Life*, Cambridge: Polity Press, 1994, pp. 81–154.
76. Cf. Jade Lindgaard and Xavier de le Porte, *Le Nouveau B.A.-BA du BHL: enquête sur le plus grand intellectuel français*, Paris: La Découverte, 2011.
77. Cf. Peter Novick, *The Holocaust in American Life*, Boston: Houghton Mifflin, 1999, p. 8.
78. Ibid., p. 239.
79. Hannah Arendt, 'A Christian Word About the Jewish Question' (1942), in *The Jewish Writings*, p. 162. Less radically, Alain Badiou has defined this attitude as a harmful form of 'nominal sacralization'; *Circonstances 3. Portées du mot 'juif'*, Paris: Lignes, 2005, p. 11. (See also 'The Infinite, the Universal, and the Name "Jew"', in Alain Badiou and Jean-Claude Milner, *Controversies: Politics and Philosophy in Our Time*, Cambridge: Polity, 2014, pp. 71–107. – Translator.)
80. Yitzhak Laor, *Le nouveau philosémitisme européen*, Paris: La Fabrique, 2007, p. 34.
81. Slzekine, *Le siècle juif*, p. 50.
82. Eric Hobsbawm, 'Benefits of Diaspora', *London Review of Books*, no. 20, 2005, pp. 16–19.

83. David Landes, *The Wealth and Poverty of Nations: Why Some Are So Rich and Some So Poor*, New York: W. W. Norton, 1999.
84. Bernard Lewis, *What Went Wrong? The Clash Between Islam and Modernity in the Middle East*, New York: Harper Perennial, 2003.
85. Cf. Ruth Wisse, *Jews and Power*, New York: Schocken Books, 2007.
86. Cf. Domenico Losurdo, *Il linguaggio dell'impero; lessico dell'ideologia Americana*, Bari: Laterza, 2007, p. 261.

Chapter 4

1. Hannah Arendt, 'On Humanity in Dark Times: Thoughts about Lessing' (1959), in *Men in Dark Times*, New York: Harvest Books, 1970, pp. 3–32.
2. Hannah Arendt and Karl Jaspers, *Correspondence 1926–1969*, New York: Harcourt Brace Jovanovich, 1992, p. 31.
3. As archetypes of these two opposing interpretations, cf. the respective books of Richard Wolin, *Heidegger's Children*, Princeton: Princeton University Press, 2001, ch. 3, pp. 30–69 and Jacques Taminiaux, *Arendt et Heidegger. La fille de Thrace et le penseur professionel*, Paris: Payot, 1992. For an overall assessment, see Dana R. Villa, *Arendt and Heidegger: The Fate of the Political*, Princeton: Princeton University Press, 1996.
4. Hannah Arendt, 'What Is Existential Philosophy?', in *Essays in Understanding 1930–1954*, New York: Schocken Books, 1994, p. 178.
5. Hannah Arendt, *Denktagebuch (1950–1973)*, Munich: Piper, 2002; see also *Essays in Understanding 1930–1954* (ed. J. Kohn), New York: Harcourt Brace, 1994, pp. 361–2.
6. Hannah Arendt, 'Martin Heidegger at Eighty', *New York Review of Books*, 21 October 1971.
7. On Arendt's life and intellectual formation, see in particular Elisabeth Young-Bruehl, *Hannah Arendt. For Love of the World*, New Haven and London: Yale University Press, 1982.
8. Written in the 1930s, this book would only be published after the war: Hannah Arendt, *Rahel Varnhagen: The Life of a Jewess*, London: East and West Library, 1958.
9. Max Weber, *Ancient Judaism*, New York: Free Press, 1967. See also Efraim Shmueli, 'The "Pariah-People" and its "Charismatic Leadership": A Revaluation of Max Weber's *Ancient Judaism*', *Proceedings of the American Academy for Jewish Research*, no. 36, 1968; Arnaldo Momigliano, 'Considerazioni sulla definizione weberiana degli ebrei come religion paria', in *Pagine ebraiche*, Turin: Einaudi, 1987, pp. 181–8.
10. Bernard Lazare, *Job's Dungheap*, New York: Schocken, 1948.

11. Cf. Nelly Wilson, *Bernard Lazare*, Paris: Albin Michel, 1985, p. 327. See Hannah Arendt, 'Herzl and Lazare', in *The Jewish Writings*, New York: Schocken Books, 2007, pp. 338–42.
12. Cf. the texts from 1933 collected in Hans-Joachim Schoeps, *'Bereit für Deutschland!' Der Patriotismus deutscher Juden und der Nationalsozialismus. Frühe Schriften 1930 bis 1939. Eine Dokumentation*, Berlin: Haude & Spener, 1970. Also cf. Enzo Traverso, *The Jews and Germany: From the 'Judeo-German Symbiosis' to the Memory of Auschwitz*, Lincoln: University of Nebraska Press, 1995, pp. 86–7.
13. Cf. Saul Friedländer, *Nazi Germany and the Jews: The Years of Persecution 1933–1939*, New York: HarperCollins, 1997, p. 21. On the relationship between the young Hannah Arendt and Kurt Blumenfeld during the Weimar republic, cf. Young-Bruehl, *Hannah Arendt*, pp. 70–4.
14. Hannah Arendt, 'The Jew as Pariah: A Hidden Tradition', in *The Jewish Writings*, pp. 275–97.
15. Arendt, *Men in Dark Times*, p. 13. See also her letter to Jaspers of 7 September 1952 in Arendt and Jaspers, *Correspondence 1926–1969*, p. 200.
16. Franz Kafka, *The Castle*, quoted by Arendt in 'The Jew as Pariah', p. 290.
17. Arendt, *Men in Dark Times*, p. 13.
18. Arendt, *The Origins of Totalitarianism*, London: Deutsch, 1986, p. 298.
19. Eleni Varikas, *Les rebuts du monde. Figures du paria*, Paris: Stock, 2007, p. 76.
20. Lazare, *Job's Dungheap*, p. 44.
21. Arendt, *The Origins of Totalitarianism*, p. 290.
22. Hannah Arendt, 'The Jewish Army – The Beginning of Jewish Politics?', in *The Jewish Writings*, p. 137. Arendt's italics.
23. Hannah Arendt, 'The So-called Jewish Army', in *The Jewish Writings*, p. 160.
24. Hannah Arendt, 'Ceterum Censeo…', in *Vor Antisemitismus ist man nur noch auf dem Monde sicher. Beiträge für die deutsch-jüdische Emigrantenzeitung 'Aufbau' in den Jahren 1941 bis 1945*, Munich: Piper, 2000, p. 31.
25. Arendt's analyses of Zionism are collected in the second part of *The Jewish Writings*. See also Richard J. Bernstein, *Hannah Arendt and the Jewish Question*, Cambridge: Polity, 1996, pp. 101–22 and Martine Leibovici, *Hannah Arendt, une juive*, Paris: Desclée de Brouwer, 1988, pp. 365–421.
26. Cf. Hannah Arendt and Gershom Scholem, *Der Briefwechsel*, Frankfurt: Jüdische Verlag/Suhrkamp, 2010, pp. 91–9.
27. Cf. Wilson, *Bernard Lazare*, pp. 298–338.

28. Hannah Arendt, 'Zionism Reconsidered', in *The Jewish Writings*, pp. 343–72.
29. Arendt, *The Origins of Totalitarianism*, p. 290. See on this subject the interesting remarks of Amnon Raz-Krakotzkin, 'Arendt, Benjamin, Scholem et le binationalisme', in *Exil et souveraineté. Judaïsme, sionisme et pensée binationale*, Paris: La Fabrique, 2007, pp. 158–87.
30. Arendt and Scholem, *Der Briefwechsel*, pp. 109–10.
31. Hannah Arendt, 'The Crisis of Zionism', in *The Jewish Writings*, pp. 334–5.
32. Otto Bauer, *The Question of Nationalities and Social Democracy*, Ann Arbor: University of Minnesota Press, 2000. This affinity has been discussed by Gabriel Piterberg, 'Zion's Rebel Daughter: Hannah Arendt on Palestine and Politics', *New Left Review*, no. 2/48, 2007, p. 50. See also Simon Doubnov, *Lettres sur le judaïsme ancient et nouveau* (ed. Renée Poznanski), Paris: Éditions du Cerf, 1989.
33. Hannah Arendt, 'We Refugees', in *The Jewish Writings*, pp. 264–5. Theodor Adorno, *Minima Moralia: Reflections from Damaged Life*, London: Verso, 2006, esp. p. 26.
34. Karl Mannheim, *Ideology and Utopia; An Introduction to the Sociology of Knowledge*, Eastford: Martino Fine Books, 2015.
35. Hannah Arendt, 'The Image of Hell' (1946), in *Essays in Understanding*, p. 198.
36. On the German-Jewish exile faced with the Shoah, cf. Enzo Traverso, *L'histoire déchirée. essai sur Auschwitz et les intellectuels*, Paris: Éditions du Cerf, 1997.
37. This is how she put it in a postwar interview: Hannah Arendt, 'What Remains? The Language Remains', in *Essays in Understanding*, p. 14.
38. Arendt, *The Origins of Totalitarianism*, p. 296.
39. Hannah Arendt, *The Promise of Politics*, New York: Schocken, 2007.
40. Martin Heidegger, *Being and Time*, New York: Harper Perennial, 2009, sections 25 and 26. On the influence of this concept of Arendt, see Syla Benhabib, *The Reluctant Modernism of Hannah Arendt*, Lanham: Rowman & Littlefield, pp. 106–22.
41. See in particular Hannah Arendt and Heinrich Blücher, *Within Four Walls: The Correspondence between Hannah Arendt and Heinrich Blücher, 1936–1938*, New York: Harcourt, 2000, esp. pp. 234, 271.
42. Hannah Arendt, 'The Ex-Communists' (1953), in *Essays in Understanding*, pp. 391–400.
43. Isaac Deutscher, 'The Ex-Communist's Conscience', in *Marxism, Wars and Revolutions: Essays from Four Decades*, London: Verso, 1984, pp. 49–59.

44. Arendt, *The Origins of Totalitarianism*, p. 299.
45. Ibid., p. 221.
46. Carl Friedrich and Zbigniev Brzezinski, *Totalitarian Democracy and Autocracy*, Cambridge, MA: Harvard University Press, 1956.
47. On the metamorphoses of the concept of totalitarianism during the Cold War years, see in particular the introduction to Enzo Traverso (ed.), *Le Totalitarisme. Le XXe siècle en débat*, Paris: Le Seuil, 2001, pp. 51–70.
48. Hannah Arendt, *Eichmann in Jerusalem*, London: Penguin, 2006. For a reconstruction of the polemics aroused by this essay, cf. in particular the studies collected in Steven E. Aschheim (ed.), *Hannah Arendt in Jerusalem*, Berkeley: University of California Press, 2001; Gary Smith (ed.), *Hannah Arendt Revisited: 'Eichmann in Jerusalem' und die Folgen*, Frankfurt: Suhrkamp, 2000, as well as the publications by Richard Bernstein and Martine Leibovici cited above.
49. See Scholem's letters to Arendt of 23 June and 12 August 1963 in Arendt and Scholem, *Der Briefwechsel*, pp. 429, 451. On this correspondence, see above all the illuminating study by Stéphane Moses, 'Das Recht zu urteilen: Hannah Arendt, Gershom Scholem und der Eichmann-Prozess', in Smith (ed.), *Hannah Arendt Revisited*, pp. 78–92.
50. Arendt, *Eichmann in Jerusalem*, p. 49.
51. Arendt and Jaspers, *Correspondence 1926–1969*, p. 564.
52. Arendt, *Men in Dark Times*, p. 18.
53. See Arendt's letter to Scholem of 24 July 1963 in *Der Briefwechsel*.
54. Arendt, *Eichmann in Jerusalem*, pp. 7 and 252 ff.
55. See Aleida Assmann, *Construction de la mémoire nationale. Une brève histoire de la notion de Bildung*, Paris: Éditions de la Maison des sciences de l'homme, 1994.
56. Arendt and Jaspers, *Correspondence*, p. 30.
57. Hannah Arendt, *The Human Condition*, Chicago: University of Chicago Press, 1958, p. 50. Elsewhere, she defines the public sphere as the place where 'Being and Appearing coincide' (*The Life of the Mind*, New York: Harcourt, Brace & Jovanovich, 1978, p. 19).
58. Benhabib, *The Reluctant Modernism of Hannah Arendt*, pp. 125–6, 199–200. On Arendt's conception of the public sphere, see also Simona Forti, *Hannah Arendt tra filosofia e politica*, Milan: Mondadori, 2006, pp. 277–87, and the entire first part of André Enegren, *La pensée politique de Hannah Arendt*, Paris: PUF, 1984.
59. Jürgen Habermas, *The Structural Transformation of the Public Sphere: An Inquiry into a Category of Bourgeois Society*, Cambridge, MA: MIT Press, 1991 and *The Theory of Communicative Action* (2 vols), Boston: Beacon Press, 1985.

60. Hannah Arendt, 'Totalitarian Imperialism: Reflections on the Hungarian Revolution', *Journal of Politics*, vol. 20, no. 1, 1958, pp. 5–43 and 'A Heroine of Revolution', *New York Review of Books*, 6 October 1966. On May 1968, see in particular Hannah Arendt and Mary McCarthy, *Between Friends: The Correspondence of Hannah Arendt and Mary McCarthy 1949–1975*, New York: Harcourt & Brace, 1995, pp. 219–27. (On 27 June 1968, Arendt wrote to Daniel Cohn-Bendit, whose parents she had known in Paris in the 1930s, to express her support.)
61. These three concepts form the organizing principle of *The Human Condition*.
62. On Arendt's contradictory relationship to the work of Burke, which she initially saw as an intellectual matrix of totalitarianism, but subsequently drew on for some themes in her critique of revolution, cf. Domenico Losurdo, 'Hannah Arendt e l'analisis delle rivoluzioni', in Roberto Esposito (ed.), *La pluralità irrappresentabile. Il pensiero politico di Hannah Arendt*, Urbino: Quattroventi, 1987, pp. 139–53.
63. Hannah Arendt, *On Revolution*, New York: Viking, 1963. On Arendt's analysis of revolution, cf. Anne Amiel, *La Non-Philosophie de Hannah Arendt*, Paris: PUF, 2001.
64. Cf. Eric Hobsbawm, 'Hannah Arendt on Revolution', in *Revolutionaries*, London: Weidenfeld & Nicolson, 1974, pp. 201–8.
65. See in particular Martin Jay, 'The Political Existentialism of Hannah Arendt', in *Permanent Exiles: Essays on the Intellectual Migration from Germany to America*, New York: Columbia University Press, 1986, pp. 237–56.
66. Hannah Arendt, 'Reflections on Little Rock', *Dissent*, no. 1, 1959, p. 51.

Chapter 5

1. Pierre-André Taguieff, *La force du préjugé*, Paris: La Découverte, 1988.
2. See Denis Sieffert, 'Antisémitisme. Entre réalité et manipulations', in *Antisémitisme. Intolérable chantage*, Paris: La Découverte, 2003, pp. 11–23.
3. Léon Poliakov, *Histoire de l'antisémitisme* (1955), Paris: Calmann-Lévy, 1981 (2 vols). For a reasoned critique of this approach, cf. Detlev Claussen, *Grenzen der Aufklärung. Zur gesellschaftlichen Geschichte des modernen Antisemitismus*, Frankfurt: Fischer, 1987. For a typological distinction, see Domenico Losurdo, 'Antiguidaismo, giudeofobia, antisemitismo', *I Viaggi de Erodoto*, no. 38–39, 1999, pp. 139–60.
4. Renaud Camus, *La campagne de France. Journal 1994*, Paris: Fayard, 2000, p. 48.

5. *La Stampa*, 5 April 2003.
6. Sergio Romano, *Lettera a un amico ebreo*, Milan: Longanesi, 1997, p. 235.
7. The pieces of this debate are collected in *Die Walser-Bubis Debatte. Eine Dokumentation*, Frankfurt: Suhrkamp, 1999. See also Heinrich Treitschke, 'Unsere Aussichten' (1879), in Walter Böhlich (ed.), *Der Berliner Antisemitismusstreit*, Frankfurt: Insel, 1988, p. 13.
8. Cf. Antonio Carioti, 'La lunga ambiguità. Neofascismo e antisemitismo nell'Italia repubblicana', in Marie-Anne Matard-Bonucci, Marcello Flores, Simon Levis-Sullam and Enzo Traverso (ed.), *Storia della Shoah in Italia*, Turin: UTET, vol. 2, 2010, pp. 267–86.
9. Cf. Pierre Birnbaum, *Un mythe politique. La 'République juive' de Léon Blum à Mendès France*, Paris: Fayard, 1988, pp. 194–5.
10. Cf. Eric Alterman, 'Dominique Strauss-Kahn and the French Anti-Semitism Myth', *Daily Beast*, 19 May 2011.
11. Cf. Pierre Vidal-Naquet, *Les asssassins de la mémoire*, Paris: La Découverte, 1995.
12. Cf. Michel Dreyfus, *L'antisémitisme à gauche. Histoire d'un paradoxe, de 1830 à nos jours*, Paris: La Découverte, 2009.
13. Cf. Michel Wieviorka, *L'antisémitisme est-il de retour?*, Paris: Larousse, 2008, pp. 50–3.
14. Cf. Patricia Touranchou, 'La voix de la haine', *Libération*, 10 July 2012.
15. Michel Wieviorka, *La tentation anti-Sémite. Haine des juifs dans la France d'aujourd'hui*, Paris: Robert Laffont, 2005, p. 181.
16. Ibid., p. 131.
17. *Le Monde*, 23 April 2002. See Daniel Lindenberg, 'L'"islam" et "les Arabes" vus par les "défenseurs d'Israël', in *Antisémitisme. L'intolérable chantage*, Paris: La Découverte, 2003, p. 47.
18. Cf. Pierre-André Taguieff, *La nouvelle judéophobie*, Paris: Mille et une nuits, 2002; Pascal Bruckner, *La tyrannie de la pénitence*, Paris: Grasset, 2006, pp. 39–40. See on this subject Pascal Boniface, *Les intellectuels faussaires. Le triomphe médiatique des experts en mensonge*, Paris: Jean-Claude Gawsewitch Éditeur, 2011, p. 60.
19. Alexandre Adler, quoted in Éric Hazan, *LQR. LapPropagande du quotidien*, Paris: Raisons d'agir, 2006, p. 95.
20. On Jabotinski, cf. Walter Laqueur, A *History of Zionism: From the French Revolution to the Establishment of Israel*, New York: Schocken, 2003, pp. 338–73; on Amin al-Husseini, Nazism and the Holocaust, cf. Gilbert Achcar, *The Arabs and the Holocaust; the Arab-Israeli War of Narratives*, London: Picador, 2011, pp. 131–76.
21. Primo Levi, *Conversazioni e interviste 1963–1987*, Turin: Einaudi, 1997, p. 298.

22. Claude Lanzmann, 'Sans ambiguïté', *Le Monde*, 5 November 2001.
23. Tariq Ali, *The Clash of Fundamentalisms: Crusades, Jihads and Modernity*, London: Verso, 2003.
24. Dan Diner, *Der Krieg der Erinnerungen und die Ordnung der Welt*, Berlin: Rotbuch Verlag, 1991.
25. Cf. Jean Birnbaum, *Les maoccidents. Un néoconservatisme à la française*, Paris: Stock, 2009. ('*Maorassien*' after Maurras, and '*maoccident*' after the fascist student movement Occident. – Translator.)
26. Shmuel Trigano, *L'idéal démocratique à l'épreuve de la Shoah*, Paris: Odile Jacob, 2000, pp. 205–7; Jean-Claude Milner, *Les penchants criminels de l'Europe démocratique*, Lausanne: Verdier, 2003.
27. On this debate, cf. Robert Kurz, *Die anti-deutsche Ideologie*, Münster: UNRAST-Verlag, 2003 and Anne Joly, 'Le phénomène *antideutsche*. Une singularité de la gauche radicale allemande', *La Revue des Livres*, no. 6, July–August 2012, pp. 76–80.
28. Jean-Yves Camus, 'Du fascisme au national-populisme. Métamorphoses de l'extrême droite en Europe', *Le Monde diplomatique*, May 2002.
29. Louis Chevalier, *Classes laborieuses et classes dangereuses* (1958), Paris: Perrin, 2007.
30. Cf. Michel Foucault, *The Archaeology of Knowledge*, New York: Vintage, 1982, pp. 129–30. On the concept of the anti-Jewish archive, cf. Simon Levis Sullam, *L'archivio antiebraico. Il linguaggio dell'antisemitismo moderno*, Rome-Bari: Laterza, 2008, pp. 10–15.
31. Shlomo Sand, 'From Judeophobia to Islamophobia: Nation-building and the Construction of Europe', *Jewish Quarterly*, no. 215, 2010, http://jewishquarterly.org/2010/07/from-judaeophobia-to-islamophobia/.
32. Edward Said, *Orientalism*, New York: Vintage, 1979, p. 286.
33. Yitzhak Laor, *Le nouveau philosémitisme européen*, Paris: La Fabrique, 2007, p. 34.
34. Oriana Fallaci, *The Rage and Pride*, New York: Rizzoli, 2002.
35. Alain Finkielkraut, *Le point*, 24 May 2002. See ibid., p. 53.
36. Alain Finkielkraut, *Au nom de l'Autre. Réflexions sur l'antisémitisme qui vient*, Paris: Gallimard, 2003, p. 20, original emphases.
37. Wieviorka, *L'antisémitisme est-il de retour?*, pp. 125–6.

Chapter 6

1. Ilan Halévi, *Question juive. La tribu, la loi, l'espace*, Paris: Éditions de Minuit, 1981, p. 181.
2. Cf. Shlomo Sand, *The Invention of the Jewish People*, London: Verso, 2009.

3. Dan Diner, 'Cumulative Contingency: Historicizing legitimacy in Israeli Discourse', in *Beyond the Conceivable. Studies on Germany, Nazism and the Holocaust*, Berkeley: University of California Press, 2000, pp. 201–17.
4. By the time of independence, the Jewish population of Palestine had grown from 174,610 in 1931 to 543,000 in 1946 and 716,700 in 1948.
5. Arno J. Mayer, *Ploughshares into Swords: From Zionism to Israel*, London: Verso, 2008, p. 196.
6. Quoted in Antonella Salomoni, *L'Unione Sovietica e la Shoah. Genocidio, resistenza, rimozione*, Bologna: Il Mulino, 2008, p. 255.
7. Ibid., p. 256.
8. Theodor Herzl, *The Jewish State*, CreateSpace, 2013, p. 45. On the origins of the movement, see Walther Laqueur, *History of Zionism: From the French Revolution to the Establishment of Israel*, New York: Schocken, 2003 and Georges Bensoussan, *Une histoire intellectuelle et politique du sionisme*, Paris: Fayard, 2001.
9. Ahad Haam, 'Nous allons vers une guerre difficile...' (1891), in Denis Charbit (ed.), *Sionismes. Textes fondamentaux*, Paris: Albin Michel, 1998, p. 394.
10. Hannah Arendt, 'To Save the Jewish Homeland', in *The Jewish Writings*, New York: Schocken Books, 2007, pp. 396–7.
11. Mayer, *Ploughshares into Swords*, p. 26. On Israeli historiography, cf. Dominique Vidal, *Comment Israël expulsa les Palestiniens. Les nouveaux acquis de l'histoire (1945–1949)*, Paris: Éditions de l'Atélier, 2007.
12. Benny Morris, *Righteous Victims: A History of the Zionist-Arab Conflict, 1881–1999*, New York: Vintage, 1999, p. 257.
13. See his interview with the Israeli newspaper *Haaretz*, in Benny Morris, 'On Ethnic Cleansing', *New Left Review*, no. 2/26, 2004, pp. 37–51.
14. Ilan Pappe, 'The Phony War and the Real War Over Palestine: May 1948', in *The Ethnic Cleansing of Palestine*, Oxford: Oneworld Publications, 2007, ch. 6.
15. Mayer, *Ploughshares into Swords*, p. 226.
16. Rashid Khalidi, *Palestinian Identity: The Construction of Modern National Consciousness*, New York: Columbia University Press, 2009.
17. Perry Anderson, 'Scurrying Towards Bethlehem', *New Left Review*, no. 2/10, 2001, p. 13.
18. Ella Shohat, *Le sionisme du point de vue de ses victimes juives. Les juifs orientaux en Israël*, Paris: La Fabrique, 2006.
19. Morris, *Righteous Victims*, p. 259.
20. Cf. Shohat, *Le sionisme du point de vue de ses victimes juives*; Gabriel Piterberg, *The Returns of Zionism: Myths, Politics and Scholarship in Israel*, London: Verso, 2008.

21. Pappe, 'The Memoricide of the Nakba', in *Ethnic Cleansing of Palestine*, ch. 10.
22. Cf. David Biale, *Power and Powerlessness in Jewish History*, New York: Schocken, 1986, p. 146.
23. Idith Zertal, *La nation et la mort. La Shoah dans le discours et la politique d'Israël*, Paris: La Découverte, 2008. Cf. Benedict Anderson, *Imagined Communities*, London: Verso, 1983.
24. See George L. Mosse, 'Max Nordau, le libéralisme et le "nouveau juif "', in Delphine Bechtel, Dominique Bourel and Jacques Le Rider (ed.), *Max Nordau 1849–1923*, Paris: Éditions du Cerf, 1996, pp. 11–29.
25. Zertal, *La nation et la mort*, ch. 1.
26. Ibid., p. 49.
27. Abraham B. Yehoshua, *Pour une normalité juive*, Paris: Liana Levi, 1998. See on this subject Yitzhak Laor, *Le nouveau philosémitisme européen*, Paris: La Fabrique, 2007, ch. 4.
28. David Vital, *A People Apart: The Jews in Europe, 1789–1939*, Oxford: OUP, 1999, p. 444.
29. Quoted in Zertal, *La nation et la mort*, p. 156. For a synthesis of this subject, cf. Annette Wieviorka, *Le Procès Eichmann*, Brussels: Complexe, 1999.
30. Hannah Arendt and Gershom Scholem, *Der Briefwechsel*, Frankfurt: Jüdische Verlag/Suhrkamp, 2010, pp. 428–59.
31. Quote in Zertal, *La nation et la mort*, p. 162.
32. Dan Diner, 'Zwischen den Zeiten', in *Gedächtniszeiten. Über politische und andere Geschichten*, Munich: C. H. Beck, 2003.
33. Amnon Raz-Krakotzkin, *Exil et souveraineté. Judaïsme, sionisme et pensée binationale*, Paris: La Fabrique, 2007, p. 191.
34. Zeev Sternhell, *The Founding Myths of Israel: Nationalism, Socialism, and the Making of the Jewish State*, Princeton: Princeton University Press, 1997, p. 72.
35. Cf. David Biale, *Not in the Heavens: The Tradition of Jewish Secular Thought*, Princeton: Princeton University Press, 2011, p. 134.
36. Cf. Biale, *Power and Powerlessness in Jewish History*, pp. 154–5.
37. Mayer, *Ploughshares into Swords*, p. xiii.

Chapter 7

1. Émile Durkheim, *Elementary Forms of Religious Life*, Oxford: OUP, p. 161.
2. Cf. Jean-Claude Monod, *La querelle de la sécularisation de Hegel à Blumenberg*, Paris: Vrin, 2002.

NOTES

3. Raymond Aron, 'L'avenir des religions séculières' (1944), in *Histoire et politique. Textes et témoignages*, Paris: Juillard, 1985, p. 370.
4. Cf. Éric Voegelin, *Les religions politiques* (1938), Paris: Éditions du Cerf, 1994.
5. On the distinction between political religions and civil religions, cf. Emilio Gentile, *Politics as Religion*, Princeton: Princeton University Press, 2006.
6. Cf. Mona Ozouf, 'Religion révolutionnaire', in François Furet and Mona Ozouf (ed.), *Dictionnaire critique de la Révolution française. Institutions et créations*, Paris: Flammarion, 1992, pp. 311–28.
7. Cf. Benedict Anderson, *Imagined Communities*, London: Verso, 1983.
8. Cf. Robert N. Bellah's classic study, 'Civil Religion in America', *Dedalus*, no. 96/1, 1967, pp. 1–21; see also Emilio Gentile, *La democrazia di Dio. La religione Americana nell'era dell'impero e del terrore*, Rome-Bari: Laterza, 2006.
9. Cf. Peter Novick, *The Holocaust in American Life*, Boston: Houghton Mifflin, 1999, pp. 198–9.
10. Jean Améry, *At the Mind's Limits: Contemplations by a Survivor on Auschwitz and the Third Reich*, Bloomington: Indiana University Press, 2009.
11. Cf. for example the essays by Richard L. Rubenstein, 'Religion and the Uniqueness of the Holocaust', and Steven T. Katz, 'The Uniqueness of the Holocaust: The Historical Dimension', in Alan S. Rosenbaum (ed.), *Is the Holocaust Unique? Perspectives on Comparative Genocide*, Boulder: Westview Press, 1996, pp. 11–18 and 19–28.
12. Claude Lanzmann, 'Hier ist kein Warum', in *Au sujet de* Shoah. *Le film de Claude Lanzmann*, Paris: Belin, 1990, p. 279. Cf. Primo Levi, *If This is a Man*, New York: Vintage, 1993, p. 35.
13. Primo Levi, *The Drowned and the Saved*, New York: Vintage, 1989, p. 83.
14. François Azouvi, *Le mythe du grand silence. Auschwitz, les français, la mémoire*, Paris: Fayard, 2012.
15. Annette Wieviorka, *L'ere du témoin*, Paris: Plon, 1998.
16. Cf. Primo Levi, 'Il sistema periodico', in *Opere I*, Turin: Einaudi, 1997, p. 932.
17. Ferdinando Camon, *Conversations avec Primo Levi*, Paris: Gallimard, 1991, p. 49.
18. Theodor W. Adorno, *Negative Dialectics*, London: Bloomsbury, 1981, p. 365.
19. Jürgen Habermas, 'Eine Art Schadensabwicklung. Die apologetischen Tendenzen in der deutschen Zeitgeschichtsschreibung', in *Historikerstreit*.

Die Dokumentation der Kontroverse um die Einzigartigkeit de nationalsozialistischen Judenvernichtung, Munich: Piper, 1987, p. 75.
20. Novick, *The Holocaust in American Life*, pp. 273–4. The concept of lachrymose history goes back to Salo W. Baron, 'Ghetto and Emancipation: Shall we Revise the Traditional View?' (1928), in Leo W. Schwartz (ed.), *The Menorah Treasury*, Philadelphia: Jewish Publication Society of America, 1964, pp. 50–63.
21. Esther Benbassa, *La souffrance comme identité*, Paris: Fayard, 2007.
22. Ibid., pp. 96, 114.
23. Emil Fackenheim, *Penser après Auschwitz*, Paris: Éditions du Cerf, 1986. See Benbassa, *La souffrance comme identité*, pp. 149–51.
24. Ibid., p. 164.
25. On the genealogy of this concept, cf. Giorgio Agamben, *What is an Apparatus? and Other Essays*, Stanford: Stanford University Press, 2009.
26. On the French case, cf. Sévane Garibian, 'Pour une lecture juridique des quatre lois "mémorielles"', *Esprit*, July 2006, pp. 158–73.
27. Jean-Michel Chaumont, *La concurrence des victimes*, Paris: La Découverte, 1997.
28. *Le Monde*, 12 December 2005. The first warning against the consequences of the Gayssot law, which punished Holocaust denial, was launched by Madeleine Rebérioux, 'Le génocide, le juge et l'historien', *L'Histoire*, no. 138, 1990, pp. 92–4. In January 2007, a similar warning was launched by Italian historians (cf. 'Contro il negazionismo, per la libertà della ricerca storica', www.sissco.it).
29. (These 'suitcase carriers' were French activists who helped the Algerian struggle by carrying money and documents. – Translator.)
30. Améry, *At the Mind's Limits*, p. 30.
31. Henri Alleg, *The Question*, Bison Books, 2006, p. 23. See also Dan Diner, 'Verschobene Erinnerung. Jean Amérys *Die Tortur* wiedergelesen', *Mittelweg 36*, Heft 2, 2012, pp. 21–7.
32. André Glucksmann, 'Pourquoi je choisis Nicolas Sarkozy', *Le Monde*, 29 January 2007.
33. Novick, *The Holocaust in American Life*, p. 279.
34. Cf. Gilbert Achcar, *The Clash of Barbarisms: The Making of the New World Disorder*, Paradigm Publishers, 2006, p. 23.

Conclusion

1. Isaiah Berlin, 'Benjamin Disraeli, Karl Marx and the Search for Identity', in *Against the Current: Essays in the History of Ideas* (ed. Henry Hardy), London: Hogarth Press, 1979, pp. 252–86.

NOTES

2. Cf. Nancy Fraser and Axel Honneth, *Redistribution or Recognition? A Political-Philosophical Exchange*, London: Verso, 2006.
3. Ibid.
4. For a new interpretation of this famous piece that puts into question its anti-Semitism, see Martin D. Yaffe, *Shylock and the Jewish Question*, Baltimore: Johns Hopkins University Press, 1999.
5. Leo Strauss, 'Introduction', in *Spinoza's Critique of Religion*, Chicago: Chicago University Press, 1997, pp. 4–5.
6. Hannah Arendt, 'On Humanity in Dark Times', *Men in Dark Times*, New York, Harcourt Brace & Company, 1968, p. 17.
7. Peter Novick, *The Holocaust in American Life*, Boston: Houghton Mifflin, 1999, p. 8.
8. Karl Marx, 'On the Jewish Question', in *Marx Engels Collected Works*, vol. 3, London: Lawrence & Wishart, 1975, pp. 146–74. On this point, see Enzo Traverso, *The Marxists and the Jewish Question*, Atlantic Highlands: Humanities Press, 1994, ch. 1.
9. Thorstein Veblen, 'The Intellectual Pre-eminence of the Jews in Europe' (1919), in Leon Ardzrooni (ed.), *Essays in Our Changing Order*, New York: Kelley, 1964, p. 222. His diagnosis coincides with that of Shlomo Sand, *The Invention of the Jewish People*, London: Verso, 2009.
10. Veblen, 'The Intellectual Pre-eminence of the Jews in Europe', p. 224.
11. Cf. Homi Bhabha, *The Location of Culture*, London: Routledge, 2004; Édouard Glissant (interviews with Lise Gauvin), *L'imaginaire des langues*, Paris: Gallimard, 2010; Edward Said, 'Traveling Theory' (1982), in *The Edward Said Reader*, London: Granta Books, 2000, pp. 195–217. On cultural hybrids and creolization, cf. two works by Nicole Lapierre, *Pensons ailleurs*, Paris: Stock, 2004 and *Causes communes. Des juifs et des noirs*, Paris: Stock, 2011.
12. Giuliano Baioni's interpretation in *Kafka, letterature ed ebraismo*, Turin: Einaudi, 1984 is articulated around this definition, taken from a letter from Franz Kafka to Max Brod of January 1918 (*Briefe 1902–1924*, Frankfurt: Fischer, 1958, p. 223).
13. Hannah Arendt, 'Walter Benjamin: 1892–1940', in Walter Benjamin (ed. H. Arendt), *Illuminations: Essays and Reflections*, New York: Schocken, 1969, p. 18.
14. Edward Said, *Humanism and Democratic Criticism*, New York: Columbia University Press, 2004.
15. Cf. Gil Z. Hochberg, 'Edward Said: The Last Jewish Intellectual. On Identity, Alterity, and the Politics of Memory', *Social Text*, vol. 87, 2006, pp. 47–66.

Index

1948 war 100–1, 103–4

Abrams, Elliot 54
action 79
Adenauer, Konrad 14, 16
Adorno, Theodor W. 4, 42, 71, 74, 119
Ahmadinejad, Mahmoud 83
Algerian independence 5, 47, 124
Alleg, Henri 124
ambiguous semantics 11, 12, 13–16
Améry, Jean 116, 124–5
Anders, Günther 62
Anderson, Perry 104–5
anti-feminism 28–30, 85
anti-Semitism
  anti-Zionism and 90–2
  decline of 3, 17, 52–3, 57–8, 82–6, 92–3
  in France 43, 84, 87–8, 90
  Islamophobia as replacement for 3, 92, 93–6, 130
  in Italy 11, 26, 44–5
  Jewish identity and 40
  during Jewish modernity 1–2, 12–13, 28–30, 36
  Judeophobia 83–6, 87–90
  nationalism and 11, 28–9, 36, 43, 84, 92, 95
  negationism 86, 123–4
  post 1950: 15, 84–6, 87–8, 92, 95
antifascism 115, 117–18
Arab-Israeli wars 55, 100–1, 103–4
Arendt, Hannah
  on Benjamin 132
  on cosmopolitanism 29

Eichmann in Jerusalem 75–7, 109–10
Gershom Scholem and 18, 62, 63, 69, 70, 75–7, 102, 109
Heidegger and 61–2, 72
on her identity 130
on Holocaust 71–2, 75–7
On Humanity in Dark Times 60–1
on pariah Judaism 12, 39, 62–7
on public sphere 77–81
on secular Judeocentrism 56–7
on totalitarianism 12, 60, 72–5
on Zionism 67–70, 71, 102–3
Arendt, Max 65
Armenian genocide 123
Aron, Raymond 43, 47, 48, 114
assimilation 22–8
At the Mind's Limits (Améry) 124–5
atheism 37
Aufbau 68
Azouvi, François 118

'banality of evil' 75–7
Baron, Salo W. 49
Ben-Gurion, David 16, 108, 109
Benbassa, Esther 121
Benhabib, Seyla 79
Benjamin, Walter 33, 42, 74, 76, 132
Berlin, Isaiah 50–2, 128
Berlin, Jewish population in 25
Bhabha, Homi 131, 132
Biale, David 106, 111
Bildung 25, 26, 28–30, 34, 78
binational state 69, 70, 102, 112
Bismarck, Otto von 2–3
Bleichröder, Gershon 17, 23–4, 28

Bloch, Ernst 42
Bloch, Marc 47
Bloom, Alan 54
Blücher, Heinrich 62, 70
Blumenfeld, Kurt 65, 75
Brit Shalom 69, 102
British Empire 49–50
Buber, Martin 32
Bund (General Jewish Labour Bund) 31–2
Burke, Edmund 74
Bush, George W. 54
Butz, Arthur 123

Camus, Renaud 84
Canetti, Elias 20
capitalism 35, 58
Castle, The (Kafka) 66
Catholic Church and anti-Semitism 11, 26, 44–5
Chagall, Marc 20, 41, 121
Chirac, Jacques 124
Churchill, Winston 1
citizenship 7, 8–9, 22, 66
    of France 7, 26, 42–3
    of Israel 16, 105
    social 80
Claims Conference 14–15
Clermont-Tonnerre, Count Stanislas-Marie-Adélaïde de 9
Cohen, Hermann 23
Cold War 73, 118
    ending of 4, 8
colonialism 58, 75, 98, 99, 100, 125
communism
    as civil religion 90, 114
    forgetting of Nazism and 118
    Jews and 1, 32, 42, 49, 55–6
    totalitarian 73, 74
confessionalization 25
conservative liberalism 50–2

conservativism 52–9, 130
Constant, Benjamin 80
cosmopolitanism 20–34, 36, 37, 38
Cukiermann, Roger 90
cultural assimilation 22–8
cultural transfer 24–8, 33–4

Dalet plan 103–4
Darmsteter, Joseph 24
Darquier de Pellepoix, Louis 19
Dasein (Heidegger) 61
Debray, Régis 17
democracy 53, 93, 97
Denktagebuch (Arendt) 61
Derenbourg, Joseph 28
Deutscher, Isaac 36–8, 52, 73
diaspora
    as exiles 109
    Israel, ties to 90, 108
    in multinational empires 10
    normalization of 3, 15, 131
    see also migration
Diner, Dan 7, 99–100, 110
Disraeli, Benjamin 46, 128
Dohm, Wilhelm von 23
Dreyfus affair 36, 43, 47, 84, 129–30
Drumont, Édouard 84
Dubnov, Simon 39
Durkheim, Émile 28, 41, 47, 113, 114

eastern Europe
    anti-Semitism, post 1950: 92, 95
    modernity period in 7, 9, 21, 24, 25–6, 27
Edelman, Marek 108–9
Ehrenburg, Ilya 101
Eichmann in Jerusalem (Arendt) 75–7, 109–10
Eichmann trial 109–10, 117–18, 122
Einstein, Albert 20, 41

Elias, Norbert 26, 56
emancipation 7–11, 22–4, 35–6, 41–2, 79–80, 84
emigration *see* migration
Exodus (ship) 108

Fackenheim, Emil 121
Fallaci, Oriana 96–7
far right movements 92–7
fascism 44–5
   decline of 92–3
   early Jewish support of 44, 45, 65, 90
   in eastern Europe 96–7
   see also Holocaust
Fini, Gianfranco 85, 93
Finkielkraut, Alain 96
First World War 116
Fofana, Youssef 87
Forattini, Giorgio 85
Fortini, Franco 55
Fortuyn, Pim 93
Forverts 31
France
   anti-negationist laws in 123–4
   anti-Semitism in 43, 84, 87–8, 90; decline of 85–6, 93
   Islamophobia in 95
   Judaeaphobia in 87–8
   modernity period in 7, 10–11, 26, 27–8, 42–3, 45, 46–8, 84
   nationalism of Jews (towards France) 43
Franco-Prussian war 23–4
Frank, Adolphe 28
Frank, Anne 113
Frankel, Boris 5
Fraser, Nancy 128–9
Freikorps 45, 46
French Revolution 113, 114
Freud, Sigmund 41, 65

Friedrich the Great 51
Front National (France) 93
functionalist interpretation 103

Gans, Eduard 27
Gasperi, Alcide De 16
Gay, Peter 32
Gebhardt, Carl 40
Geiger, Abraham 24
genocide, use of term 120
   see also Holocaust
George, Stefan 45
Germany
   anti-negationist laws in 123–4
   anti-Semitism in 28–30, 85; decline of 85, 92
   exodus from during Holocaust 33–4
   Holocaust, consciousness of 14–15, 16, 119
   Islamophobia in 95
   modernity period in 10–11, 21–32, 46–8, 78
   nationalism of Jews (towards Germany) 45–6, 65
   pro-Israeli groups in 91–2
   restitution agreements with Israel 14–15, 16
Geschichte der Juden (Graetz) 27
Glissant, Édouard 131, 132
globalization 3, 15, 35–6, 93, 131–2
Glucksmann, André 125
'godless Jews' 9
Goldmann, Nahum 14
Goldstein, Moritz 26
Graetz, Heinrich 27, 121
Gramsci, Antonio 44
Gray, John 50
Great Britain 46, 49–50, 100, 101
Great War 116
Gromyko, Andrei 101

INDEX

Guttmann, Julius 28

Ha-Cohen, Jospeh 121
Haam, Ahad 101–2
Habermas, Jürgen 79, 119
Halimi, Ilan 87
Hamann, Johann Georg 51
Haskalah 27
Heidegger, Martin 61–2, 72
Helphand, Alexander Israel
    (Parvus) 31, 41
Herzl, Theodor 18, 45, 64, 99,
    129–30
Hilferding, Rudolf 22
historiography (Jewish) 12
history and law 122–5
Hobsbawm, Eric 57, 79–80, 104
Holocaust
    Arendt on 71–2, 75–7
    as civil religion 3, 15, 111, 115–27
    in collective memory 91, 107–10,
        117–20
    Israel and 16–17, 107–10, 121
    law and 122–5
    migration and axis shift due to
        7–8, 33–4, 100
    neoconservatives and 125–7
    as part of historical sequence 13
    transposition onto present 97,
        116, 118–20
    as turning point 57–8, 82
    Wiesel on 56
Horkheimer, Max 42, 63, 74
Huntington, Samuel 54
Hussein, Saddam 91
al-Husseini, Amin 90

immigration *see* migration
imperialism 2–3, 10, 48–52, 58–9,
    74, 99
infra 72–3

intellectuals
    cosmopolitanism of 20–1
    critical thought as tradition of
        3–4, 17, 57–8
    'non-Jewish Jews' as 36–42
    political right, shift to 52–9, 128
    as revolutionaries 32, 36
    scientists vs 46–8
intentionalist interpretation 103
internationalism 31–2, 41
Irving, David 123
Islamic fundamentalism 88–90
Israel
    anti-Semitism vs anti-Zionism
        90–2
    birth of 98–107
    eastern Jews in 16, 105–6
    Holocaust and 16–17, 107–10,
        121
    immigration into 8
    migration to 7–8, 99, 100
    Palestinians and 15, 69, 88, 98,
        101–5
    political theology in 110–12
    restitution agreements 14–15
Italy
    anti-Semitism in 11, 26, 44–5;
        decline of 85, 92–3
    Islamophobia in 95
    modernity period in 26, 43–5
    'state Jews' in 42, 43–5

Jabotinsky, Vladimir Zeev 90
Jakobson, Roman 42
Jewish modernity
    anti-Semitism during 1–2, 12–13,
        28–30, 36
    concept of 7–8
    cosmopolitanism 20–34
    emancipation period 7–11, 22–4,
        35–6, 41–2, 84

ending of 3–4, 17, 52–9, 82–6, 113, 128–32
'non-Jewish Jews' 35–42
'state Jews' 42–6
see also emancipation
'Jewish question' 18–19, 61, 67–8, 74, 129–30
Jitlowski, Haïm 39
John (Jean)-Paul II (Pope) 121
Judeophobia 83–6, 87–90

Kafka, Franz 22, 66, 132
Kagan, Robert 54
Kallen, Horace M. 49
Kant, Immanuel 51, 61, 76
Kantorowicz, Ernst 45
Katz, Jacob 41
Kertesz, Imre 116
Keynes, John Maynard 1–2
Khalidi, Rachid 104
King David Hotel, attack on 101
Kissinger, Henry 2–3
Klotz, Louis-Lucien 1–2
Konkret 92
Kracauer, Siegfried 33
Kramer, Martin 55–6

La question (Alleg) 124
La Rochelle, Drieu 47
Landes, David 58
Lanzmann, Claude 91, 116, 117, 121
Laor, Yitzhak (Ithak) 57, 95
laws
  Holocaust and 122–5
  individual vs collective rights 13–15
Lazare, Bernard 12, 64, 67
Le Pen, Marine 93
Lenin, Vladimir I. 1
Levi, Primo 90, 116, 117, 118, 119
Lévi-Strauss, Claude 42

Lévinas, Emmanuel 18
Lewis, Bernard 58
liberalism 43, 50–2
libertarian memory 124
liberty 78–81
Lindenberg, Daniel 40
Lloyd George, David 1–2
Lombroso, Cesare 45
Luftmenschen 22
Luxemburg, Rosa 31, 32, 38

Mannheim, Karl 41
marrano memory 124
Marranos 40
Marx, Karl 12, 30–1, 35, 38, 128, 130
Mauss, Marcel 41
Mayer, Arno J. 104
McCarthyism 53–4, 55, 73
Medem, Vladimir 14, 39
Mendelssohn, Moses 23, 27, 40, 51
Merah, Mohamed 87–8
Merchant of Venice, The (Shakespeare) 129
Mercurians 35–40
Metternich, Prince Klemens von 2
Michels, Robert 31
migration
  within Europe 24–5
  to Israel 7–8, 99, 100
  postcolonial, to Europe 89
  racism and 93–6
  to US 7–8, 21, 23, 33–4, 78
  see also diaspora
Mitteleuropa 21–2
Momigliano, Arnaldo 44
Moneta, Jakob 5
Morgenthau, Hans 54
Morris, Benny 103
Mosse, George L. 28
Munk, Solomon 28

Muskeljude 108

nation-states and exclusion 10, 11
  see also nationalism
National Front (France) 93
nationalism
  anti-Semitism and 11, 28–9, 36, 43, 84, 92, 95
  German, postwar 119
  Islamophobia and 92, 93–6
  of Jews: towards European countries 43, 45–6, 65; towards Israel 16, 70, 107
  Popper on 49–50
  see also Zionism
negationism 86, 123–4
negative liberty 78–9
neoconservativism 52–9, 130
Netherlands, far right in 93, 95
'non-Jewish Jews' 35–42
Nora, Pierre 48, 131
Novick, Peter 56, 126
Nuremberg trials 117, 122

Offenbach, Jacques 33
On Humanity in Dark Times (Arendt) 60–1
Open Society and Its Enemies, The (Popper) 49–50
Origins of Totalitarianism, The (Arendt) 60, 72–5
Ottolenghi, Giuseppe 44

pacifism 115
Pahlavi, Reza 52
Palestinian Liberation Organization 104
'Palestinian question' 8, 19
Palestinians 8, 15, 69, 88, 98, 101–5, 112
Pappe, Ilan 103, 106

pariah Judaism 12, 39, 62–7
parvenu Jews 64–5
Parvus (Alexander Israel Helphand) 31, 41
patriotism 113–14, 115
Perle, Richard 54
Pinochet, Augusto 2–3
Places of Memory (Nora) 48
political preferences of Jews 4, 52–9, 91–2
political religions 114
political theology in Israel 110–12
Popper, Karl 49–50
postfascism 92–3
Protocols of the Elders of Zion 87
Prussia *see* Germany
public sector, Jews in 1–3, 42–6
public sphere, Arendt on 77–81

racialism 84
racism 82–3, 84, 92, 93–7, 130
Radek, Karl 1, 31
Rage and the Pride, The (Fallaci) 95–6
Rathenau, Walther 28, 45–6
Raz-Krakotzkin, Amnon 111
Rechtsstaat 51
recognition 128–9
Renan, Ernest 11
republicanism 43, 78, 79–80, 115
restitution agreements 14–15
revolutionaries, Jews as 1, 3, 22, 36
Risorgimento 44
Robin, Régine 27
Romano, Sergio 85
Roth, Joseph 29–30, 33
Rothschild, Alphonse de 23–4
Roudinesco, Elisabeth 48
Rousseau, Jean-Jacques 52, 113, 126
Russia
  anti-Semitism in 25–6, 84

secularization in 27
at WWI peace negotiations 1
see also eastern Europe; USSR

sacralization 114–15
Said, Edward 4, 95, 102, 131, 132
Sand, Shlomo 95
Santen, Sal 5–6
Sarkozy, Nicolas 125
Sartre, Jean-Paul 47
Schmitt, Carl 54
Schoeps, Hans-Joachim 45
Scholem, Gershom 18, 62, 63, 69, 70, 75–7, 102, 109
Schuman, Robert 16
scientists 46–8
secular Jews 9
secularization 25, 27, 36–40, 140
Segré, Ivan 52–3
Shoah see Holocaust
shtetlakh 21
Shulsky, Abram 54
Simmel, Georg 39, 41
Simon-Nahum, Perrine 28
Singer, Isaac Bashevis 20–1
Sittlichkeit 28
Six Day War 55
Slezkine, Yuri 35–6
Social and Religious History of the Jews (Baron) 49
social emancipation 79–80
socialism 22, 31, 32, 41, 43, 55
Sonnino, Sidney 44
Soviet Union 70, 90, 101
see also Russia
Spain 40, 92
Spielberg, Steven 117
Spinoza, Baruch 38, 41
'state Jews' 42–6
Sternhell, Zeev 52, 111
Strauss-Kahn, Dominic 85–6

Strauss, Leo 53, 77, 130
Straussians 53–4
Switzerland, Islamophobia in 95

Taguieff, Pierre-André 84
Taubes, Jacob 18
'territory Jew' 48
tikkun 121
Tocqueville, Alexis de 17
torture 124
totalitarianism
    Arendt on 12, 60, 72–5
    Berlin on 52
    British Empire vs 50
    Nazi vs communist 118
    as secular religion 114
    in US political science 34
Toynbee, Arnold 11
Treitschke, Heinrich von 85
Tristan, Flora 66
Trotsky, Leon 1, 3, 12, 41, 55

United Kingdom 46, 49–50, 100, 101
United States
    Arendt on 78–9
    Baron on 49
    as defender of Israel 107
    Jewish shift to right in 53–6
    Kissinger as representative of 2–3
    migration to 7–8, 21, 23, 33–4, 78
    patriotism in 115
urbanization 10, 25
USSR 70, 90, 101
    see also Russia

Valley of Tears, The (Ha-Cohen) 121
Varikas, Eleni 66–7
Varnhagen, Rahel Levin 63–4
Veblen, Thorstein 131

INDEX

Versailles Conference (1919) 1–2
Vidal-Naquet, Pierre 4–5, 47–8
Vienna, Jewish population in 25
Vietnam-US peace treaty 2
Vital, David 109
Voltaire 51

Walser, Martin 85
'wandering Jew' 20
wars (Israeli) 55, 100–1, 103–4
Warsaw ghetto uprising 108–9
Weber, Max 12, 47, 64, 131
Weimar Republic 23, 32, 46, 53
West, concept of 58–9
West Germany *see* Germany
Wiedergutmachung agreements 14–15
Wiesel, Elie 56, 110, 117, 121
Wieviorka, Michel 88, 97
Wilders, Geert 95
Wisse, Ruth 58
Wissenschaft des Judentums 27–8
Wolfowitz, Paul 54
World of Yesterday, The (Zweig) 10
World War I 116
worldlessness 12, 66, 67, 71

Yeoshua, Avraham B. 109
Yerushalmi, Josef H. 18
Yiddish language and culture (*Yiddishkeit*)
  abandonment of 25
  Arendt and 63
  Deutscher on 39
  in eastern Europe 9–10, 26
  internationalism and 31–2
  as national culture 11
  renewal of 27

Zentralverein 65
Zertal, Idith 109
Zionism 12, 16, 98–112
  anti-Semitism vs 90–2
  Arendt on 67–70, 71
  Berlin on 50–2
  Holocaust and 107–10, 111
  Israel, birth of 98–107
  Popper on 50
  religion and 110–12
  Wisse on 58
Zunz, Leopold 27
Zur Judenfrage (Marx) 30–1
Zweig, Stefan 10, 29, 33